iPOD REPAIR
QuickSteps

About the Authors

Brandon Jones is the founder of iKaput.com, one of the fastest growing iPod repair companies in the United States. His newest business venture is Sync (synctogo.com), which promises to make life with the iPod easier. Sync's Web presence and physical locations offer many different services for iPod users, including repair, exchange, and accessories.

Marc Campbell is a technology author, graphic designer, and instructor. His popular books on computer topics have appeared around the world in eight languages.

About the Technical Editor

Guy Hart-Davis is the author of *How to Do Everything with Your iPod and iTunes, Fourth Edition* and *CNET Do-It-Yourself iPod Projects* (both published by McGraw-Hill).

iPOD REPAIR
QuickSteps

BRANDON JONES
MARC CAMPBELL

New York Chicago San Francisco
Lisbon London Madrid Mexico City
Milan New Delhi San Juan
Seoul Singapore Sydney Toronto

The McGraw·Hill Companies

Cataloging-in-Publication Data is on file with the Library of Congress

McGraw-Hill books are available at special quantity discounts to use as premiums and sales promotions, or for use in corporate training programs. For more information, please write to the Director of Special Sales, Professional Publishing, McGraw-Hill, Two Penn Plaza, New York, NY 10121-2298. Or contact your local bookstore.

Information has been obtained by McGraw-Hill from sources believed to be reliable. However, because of the possibility of human or mechanical error by our sources, McGraw-Hill, or others, McGraw-Hill does not guarantee the accuracy, adequacy, or completeness of any information and is not responsible for any errors or omissions or the results obtained from the use of such information.

iPOD REPAIR QUICKSTEPS

1234567890 CCI CCI 01987

ISBN: 978-0-07-149866-1
MHID: 0-07-149866-4

SPONSORING EDITOR / Roger Stewart

EDITORIAL SUPERVISOR / Jody McKenzie

PROJECT MANAGER / Samik Roy Chowdhury (Sam)

SERIES CREATORS AND EDITORS / Martin and Carole Matthews

ACQUISITIONS COORDINATOR / Carly Stapleton

TECHNICAL EDITOR / Guy Hart-Davis

COPY EDITOR / Lisa McCoy

PROOFREADER / Elise Oranges

INDEXER / Valerie Perry

PRODUCTION SUPERVISOR / George Anderson

COMPOSITION / International Typesetting and Composition

ILLUSTRATION / International Typesetting and Composition

SERIES DESIGN / Bailey Cunningham

ART DIRECTOR, COVER / Jeff Weeks

COVER DESIGN / Patti Lee

Contents at a Glance

Contents

Acknowledgments

Thanks to Roger Stewart, Carly Stapleton, James Kussow, and the rest of the team at McGraw-Hill, whose professional guidance and personal attention helped us to deliver the best book possible.

Thanks to Guy Hart-Davis for a great many valuable suggestions during the editing stage.

Thanks to Jody McKenzie, Lisa McCoy, Sam RC, George Anderson, and all who helped to produce this book. "We couldn't have done it without you" doesn't quite cover it.

Thanks to Neil Salkind, Linda Thornton, Heather Brown, and everyone else at Studio B for getting us going and keeping us there.

Introduction

QuickSteps books are recipe books for computer users. They answer the question "How do I...?" by providing a quick set of steps to accomplish the most common tasks with a particular program. The sets of steps are the central focus of the book. Sidebar QuickSteps provide information on how to do quickly many small functions or tasks that are in support of the primary functions. Sidebar QuickFacts supply information that you need to know about a subject. Notes, Tips, and Cautions augment the steps, but they are presented in a separate column to not interrupt the flow. Brief introductions are present, but there is minimal narrative otherwise. Many illustrations and figures, a number with callouts, are also included where they support the steps.

QuickSteps books are organized by function and the tasks needed to perform those functions. Each function is a chapter. Each task, or "How To," contains the steps needed for its accomplishment along with the relevant Notes, Tips, Cautions, and screenshots. Tasks are easy to find through:

- The Table of Contents, which lists the functional areas (chapters) and tasks in the order they are presented

- A How To list of tasks on the opening page of each chapter

- The index, which provides an alphabetical list of the terms that are used to describe the functions and tasks

- Color-coded tabs for each chapter or functional area with an index to the tabs in the Contents at a Glance

Conventions Used in this Book

iPod Repair QuickSteps uses several conventions designed to make the book easier for you to follow. Conventions used include:

- An icon in the Table of Contents and in the How To list in each chapter references a QuickSteps 🌀 or a QuickFacts 🖉 sidebar in a chapter.

- **Bold type** is used for words or objects on the screen that you are to do something with, like click **Home**, click **My eBay**, and click **Favorites**.

- *Italic type* is used for a word or phrase that is being defined or otherwise deserves special emphasis.

- <u>Underlined type</u> is used for text that you are to type from the keyboard.

- SMALL CAPITAL LETTERS are used for keys on the keyboard, such as ENTER and SHIFT.

- When you are expected to enter a command, you are told to press the key(s). If you are to enter text or numbers, you are told to type them.

How to...

Chapter 1

What Kind of iPod Do I Have?

The red one? The silver one? Does it really matter?

Actually, yes. Not so much because of the color, but because of what's inside. The iPod has been around since 2001, and already there have been multiple generations of products leveraging the power of all kinds of different (and sometimes competing) technologies. Today's iPod might work more or less the same as the classic original did, but what makes each individual generation of iPod work is surprisingly different when you get down to it.

As with anything high-tech, the closer you look, the more complicated it gets. Before you can attempt to fix your iPod, you need to know exactly what you're fixing. The parts and even the techniques that you use often change depending upon the model.

Hence, the purpose of this introductory chapter. We'll get you up to speed on what vintage iPod you're packing. You don't need a serial number, and you don't need an instruction manual. All you need is your good sense and the words and pictures herein. We discuss storage capacity, production dates, component compatibility, and other identifying features. We also touch on some of the little quirks and details that make iPod ownership less like class consciousness and more like enlightenment.

Identify Your iPod

October 23, 2001, is one for the history books. It was a Tuesday. On that day, after decades of armed resistance, the Provisional Irish Republican Army of Northern Ireland—the PIRA—announced that its members would put their guns to the ground, that they could not shoot them anymore, as Bob Dylan might have described it. (Perhaps it was getting too dark to see.) On *One Life to Live*, Nora further alienated Sam when he overheard her tell Troy that she wanted him; she meant as a doctor, but Sam assumed otherwise. And Apple released its very first iPod.

The PIRA has since ended its armed campaign. Troy was marked for murder, but Sam was accidentally killed in his place, and Nora was able to get on with her life, while the iPod has become one of the most successful consumer electronic devices ever manufactured.

The iPod has been through four or five generations, depending on how you count them (not unlike a soap opera, come to think of it). We show you how to tell them apart in the upcoming sections.

> **NOTE**
>
> "Knockin' on Heaven's Door," written and performed by Bob Dylan, came out in 1973 for the soundtrack to the film *Pat Garrett & Billy the Kid*. In two short verses, it invokes the image of a cowboy gunslinger who has lost his stomach for shooting and killing (perhaps quite literally). Countless artists have covered this song in nearly every style imaginable, from Bob Marley's reggae version to Guns N' Roses' hard-rock version to Roger Waters' paranoid version.

> **NOTE**
>
> Happy Birthday, iPod! You were born on October 23, 2001. Your sun sign is Scorpio. You have a magnetic personality. You are intense, creative, and passionate. Your ideal career paths include rock star, cult leader, poet, and confidence artist. You just missed the cutoff for Libras—October 22—so you might be a little wishy-washy.

As you probably already know, your iPod stores songs as digital files on an internal hard drive very much like the hard drive in a computer. (Later iPods, such as the iPod mini and the iPod nano, do it a bit differently, as you'll see later in this chapter.) The GB, or *gigabyte*, rating determines the amount of storage space on the drive: the larger the number, the more storage space. The more storage space, the more tunes you can keep on the iPod at a time. So, of Apple's initial iPod offerings, the 10-GB iPod had twice the storage capacity of the 5-GB iPod, but even 5 GB seemed pretty commodious in 2001.

QUICKSTEPS

DETERMINE YOUR iPOD'S STORAGE CAPACITY

Many iPods have the storage capacity of the hard drive stamped on the back. If yours doesn't, or even if it does, you can always access this information through the menu.

1. Press the **Menu** button.

2. Scroll down to the **Settings** selection.

3. Find and select the **About** menu.

This causes your iPod to return all kinds of useful information, including the number of songs stored, the total hard drive capacity, the hard drive space still available, the software version, the serial number, the model number, and (usually) the format, whether Windows or Mac.

Identify a First-Generation iPod

As we already mentioned, the first-generation iPod appeared in October 2001. It came in 5-gigabyte (GB) and 10-GB models.

One of the quickest and easiest ways to tell if you have a first-generation iPod is to look at the scroll wheel. On the first-generation iPod, the scroll wheel is mechanical—it physically moves (see Figure 1-1). No other iPod has this feature. The control buttons—Play/Pause, Menu, Forward, and Reverse—are also mechanical, and they all appear around the scroll wheel.

The first-generation iPod connects to computers and other devices through a FireWire port, which you find at the top of the unit (see Figure 1-2). Unlike later models, the first-generation iPod connects exclusively through FireWire. It does not support any other type of data connection.

Figure 1-1: **On a first-generation iPod, the scroll wheel is mechanical, and the mechanical control buttons appear around it.**

Figure 1-2: **The FireWire port is on the top of the first-generation iPod.**

NOTE

FireWire, or the Institute of Electrical & Electronics Engineers (IEEE) 1394 interface, is a method of transferring digital data very quickly. Apple developed it in the 1990s primarily for digital video and audio as a cheaper and less messy-with-cables replacement for the dominant Small Computer System Interface (SCSI, pronounced *skuzzy*) interface. As a convenience to the consumer (that's you), a single FireWire cable can serve as a power cord as well as a data connection. Hence, you can charge your iPod's battery via FireWire at the same time that you move tunes between devices.

The LCD—the *liquid crystal display*, or the iPod's screen—is in monochrome (see Figure 1-3). The first-generation iPod does not display in full color. Also, the LCD on this iPod is not backlit, and the FireWire port does not have a cover.

Identify a Second-Generation iPod

The second-generation iPod came out in July 2002 in 10-GB and 20-GB models. This iPod looks very much like the first-generation model, but it has some key differences. Perhaps most importantly, the scroll wheel on the second-generation iPod does not physically move; rather, it is touch-sensitive. (All subsequent generations of iPods include this feature.) The control buttons, however, are still mechanical. Play/Pause, Menu, Forward, and Reverse appear around the touch wheel in a similar configuration to the first-generation iPod (see Figure 1-4).

Like the first-generation iPod, the second-generation iPod connects to other devices exclusively through its FireWire port, which you find on

Figure 1-3: **The first-generation iPod's LCD is in monochrome and is not backlit.**

Figure 1-4: **A second-generation iPod has a touch-sensitive pad instead of a mechanical scroll wheel, and the mechanical control buttons appear around it.**

the top of the unit. Unlike the first-generation iPod, the FireWire port here sports a protective cover (see Figure 1-5).

Figure 1-5: *The second-generation iPod's FireWire port comes with a protective cover.*

As for the LCD of the second-generation iPod, it's in monochrome and is not backlit.

Identify a Third-Generation iPod

The third-generation iPod came out in April 2003 and eventually appeared in five different versions: 10 GB, 15 GB, 20 GB, 30 GB, and 40 GB.

The four buttons, as well as the scroll pad, are completely touch-sensitive on this iPod—no more mechanical controls. The configuration of the buttons is different here, too. They appear in a row in the middle of the iPod between the LCD and the scroll pad, and they light up (see Figure 1-6).

Figure 1-6: *The buttons on a third-generation iPod are touch-sensitive, they light up, and they appear in a row between the LCD and the scroll pad.*

The third-generation iPod is the first to have a docking port on the bottom (see Figure 1-7). This port enables you to connect the iPod to a docking station for charging or for hooking up to a sound system.

Figure 1-7: **The third-generation iPod has a docking port on the bottom.**

The LCD of the third-generation iPod is in monochrome, but it is backlit, which makes the display easier to read in the dark or under bright light.

This iPod is also FireWire-based, and you need to charge its battery through a FireWire cable, but you can *sync* (as in *synchronize*) the iPod to a computer through Universal Serial Bus (USB). Syncing means updating your iPod to match your iTunes playlists or your entire library. It's basically about connecting your iPod to your computer and loading music.

Identify a Fourth-Generation (Monochrome) iPod

July 2004 saw the release of the fourth-generation iPod in 20-GB and 40-GB models. This iPod sported a *Click Wheel* instead of buttons (see Figure 1-8), which it borrowed from the iPod mini, as you'll see a bit later

Figure 1-8: **The fourth-generation iPod has a grey-colored Click Wheel instead of separate control buttons.**

> **NOTE**
>
> USB stands for Universal Serial Bus. Like FireWire, it's a method of transferring digital data at high speeds. Also like FireWire, it provides power to the connected device through the data cable. In the second half of the 1990s, USB went through two commercial versions—1.0 and 1.1—without being able to touch FireWire's transfer rates. All that changed with the release of USB 2.0 in April 2000; USB 2.0 is comparable to and even faster than FireWire in some cases. Gradually, USB 2.0 overtook FireWire in popularity to the point that later-generation devices from Apple—the creators of FireWire, no less—offer USB ports only.

in this chapter. The Play/Pause, Menu, Forward, and Reverse functions all appear on the grey-colored disc that sits atop mechanical buttons.

The fourth-generation iPod includes the docking port from the third generation, and it expands its support of USB beyond syncing. You can fully connect a fourth-generation iPod to another device for recharge as well as data transfer by FireWire or USB. The fourth generation also saw the release of the Apple iPod from HP, or iPod + hp, as it's sometimes called, which lasted about a year in the marketplace.

The LCD of a fourth-generation iPod displays in monochrome and is backlit. The issue gets a little stickier, however, with the introduction of the iPod photo, as you'll see momentarily. To distinguish the original fourth-generation iPod from the iPod photo, you sometimes hear the unofficial name "iPod monochrome" to refer specifically to the fourth-generation monochrome model.

Identify Your iPod Photo (Fourth-Generation) Color iPod

The iPod photo with its full-color LCD and capacity for storing and displaying digital photos first appeared in October 2004 as a separate product alongside the standard fourth-generation monochrome iPod. Eventually—in June 2005, to be exact—Apple stopped making the iPod monochrome and dropped *photo* from the name of the newer product. From that point on, what had once been the iPod photo was now simply the iPod.

With the notable exception of the color LCD, the iPod photo looks identical to the fourth-generation monochrome iPod, right down to the docking port (see Figure 1-9). Despite appearances, though, the internal parts of the iPod *photo* are not compatible with those of a fourth-generation monochrome iPod. The storage capacities of the internal hard drive were different, too, with 20-GB, 30-GB, 40-GB, and 60-GB models. On a performance note, audiophiles tend to point to the iPod photo as being the best sounding of all the iPods.

LOOKING AT THE U2 SPECIAL EDITION iPOD

Hello, hello! The Apple iPod U2 Special Edition brought music fans to where the streets have no name in the name of love. It was the perfect lifestyle accessory to *How to Dismantle an Atomic Bomb*, U2's 2004 studio album, the eleventh from the band. The color scheme coordinated perfectly with *Dismantle's* album cover. Flip the iPod over, and you found signatures of all four band members—John, Paul, George, and Ringo—and an etched U2 logo. Beneath this ultra-cool exterior beats the heart of a fourth-generation monochrome iPod.

But monochrome is monochrome, while color is color. In any consumption-crazy, gadget-obsessed culture, the only thing cooler than a U2 monochrome iPod is a U2 color iPod, which also appeared as a special edition. Outside, it looks like the monochrome U2 iPod, only with a color LCD. Inside, it's an iPod photo.

If you're repairing your U2 Special Edition iPod, treat the monochrome version as a fourth-generation iPod, and treat the color version as an iPod photo.

*Figure 1-9: **The iPod photo has a color LCD, but otherwise it looks exactly like the fourth-generation monochrome iPod.***

Identify Your iPod Video (Fifth-Generation iPod)

The fifth-generation iPod, also known as the iPod video, the iPod with video, and the iPod 5G, appeared in October 2005 in 30-GB and 60-GB models. It's the first iPod to support digital video as well as digital photos and digital audio.

Identifying a fifth-generation iPod is pretty easy. Perhaps most notably, the big, 2.5-inch display on this generation of iPod is a dead giveaway (see Figure 1-10). It comes in either a black or white case with a grey Click Wheel. Just like previous generations, there is a docking port on the bottom.

QUICK**FACTS**

CONSIDERING THE NEWEST iPOD

At the time this book goes to press, the most recent iPod on the shelves is the Gen 5.5, which came out in September 2006. This model is basically the same as the 5G, but it comes in an 80-GB version and has a 30 percent brighter screen. It also does better on battery power when playing digital video, and it features a music search function.

But even more importantly than oxygen and fresh water, a host of brand new, retooled iPods is all set to come out in 2008. The iPod shuffle is slated to appear in four new colors. The iPod nano will be redesigned from the ground up. The standard iPod, also redesigned, will come bearing a new name—the iPod classic—and a completely new product, the iPod touch, a species of iPod/iPhone hybrid, will generate its very first massive quarterly sales.

We mention these facts for the sake of completeness. We don't talk about repairing the newest iPods in this book, because our precious few pages are better spent covering the older models. If you have one of these latest-and-greatest, and if it isn't working properly, the chances are good that it's still under warranty, so get your repairs made on Steve Jobs' dime.

NOTE

The Microdrive is a miniature hard drive. It was designed to fit in a CompactFlash (CF) slot, like the kind on a digital camera. IBM developed the Microdrive in 1999. Other manufacturers have since come out with their own licensed Microdrives, as well as unlicensed, Microdrive-like alternatives, which most people call *microdrives* anyway for the same reason that you call all soft paper tissues *kleenexes*, whether or not Kleenex actually makes them.

Figure 1-10: **The fifth-generation iPod has a 2.5-inch display.**

Identify Your iPod Mini

"From a marketing point of view, you don't introduce new products in August." That's what Andrew Card, the first Chief of Staff of President George W. Bush, said to the *New York Times* when asked why the Bush administration waited until September 2002 to sound the alarm against a grave and gathering threat. True to Mr. Card's insight, Apple brought out the iPod mini not in August, but in February 2004.

The iPod mini is smaller, thinner, and lighter than the already small, thin, and light iPod. Its storage capacity rivals that of first-generation iPods, although the iPod mini uses a Microdrive for its internal hard drive.

The marketplace saw two generations of iPod minis before the iPod nano knocked it into obsolescence.

Identify a First-Generation iPod Mini

The first-generation iPod mini with its 4-GB Microdrive came in five different colors: pink, green, gold, silver, and blue (see Figure 1-11). On the bottom of the iPod mini, you'll find a docking port, which works just like the one on the iPod proper.

Figure 1-11: *The first-generation iPod mini came in five different colors.*

Figure 1-12: **The storage capacity of the first-generation iPod mini is not stamped on the back.**

Unlike all the other previously released iPods, the storage capacity of the iPod mini is not stamped on the back of the unit (see Figure 1-12).

The LCD of the iPod mini is in monochrome and is backlit. The iPod mini can connect and charge through FireWire and USB.

Identify a Second-Generation iPod Mini

The iPod mini entered the second generation in February 2005 with 4-GB and 6-GB models. These look almost identical to the first generation, but there are a few tell-tale differences. First, the storage capacity of a second-generation iPod mini appears on the back of the unit (see Figure 1-13). Second, the markings on the second-generation iPod mini's Click Wheel match the color of the casing (see Figure 1-14).

NOTE

The second-generation iPod mini featured a longer battery life than the first-generation iPod mini.

NOTE

The internal parts of first- and second-generation iPod minis are not interchangeable.

*Figure 1-13: **The storage capacity of a second-generation iPod mini appears on the back of the unit.***

*Figure 1-14: **The markings on the second-generation iPod mini's Click Wheel match the color of the casing.***

The docking port is on the bottom of the unit, and the monochrome LCD is backlit. You connect the iPod mini to other devices through FireWire or USB 2.0.

Identify Your iPod Nano

In September 2005, the iPod mini joined the ranks of Intellivision, Betamax, Divx players, and standard-definition TV in the bin for technology products for whom the bell has tolled. The hip new iPod nano replaced it.

With its flash memory instead of the iPod mini's Microdrive and the color LCD instead of the mini's monochrome (and the conspicuous absence of a FireWire port),

Flash memory differs from other types of digital storage in that it is *non-volatile*, meaning that it doesn't require power to retain its stored information. It has been around since the 1980s, but it didn't really take off until the 21st century due to its being so expensive. Flash memory is generally considered to be the future of data storage in hard disk systems. The first flash-only hard drives for computers have already appeared. So have hybrid hard drives that combine flash with conventional volatile storage methods.

the iPod nano exuded todayness and set a whole new gotta-have-it itch upon consumers. The iPod nano product line has since gone through two generations.

Identify a First-Generation iPod Nano

The first-generation iPod nano came in three models—1 GB, 2 GB, and 4 GB—and two colors: white with a grey Click Wheel and black (see Figure 1-15).

Figure 1-15: *The first-generation iPod nano came in two colors.*

Figure 1-16: *Find the first-generation iPod nano's docking port—as well as the audio jack—on the bottom of the unit.*

The first-generation iPod nano incorporates the same style Click Wheel as the previous iPod mini models. On the bottom of the unit, you find the docking port plus the audio jack (see Figure 1-16). Not everyone is happy with Apple for putting the audio jack on the bottom, because it isn't the most convenient place for a headphone connection, although it makes better sense for certain kinds of carrying cases and accessories.

The first-generation iPod nano discontinued iPod's four-year tradition of FireWire support. USB is now the sole method of connecting the iPod nano to other devices. You can charge your nano's battery via FireWire, but you get a pop-up window that informs you that you can't make a data connection.

Identify a Second-Generation iPod Nano

The second-generation iPod nano appeared in September 2006 in a spectrum of colors and storage capacities. The 2-GB model came in silver; the 4-GB model came in silver, green, blue, pink, and red; and the 8-GB model came in black and red (see Figure 1-17).

Figure 1-17: The second-generation iPod nano appeared in a variety of colors, depending on the storage capacity.

Like the first-generation iPod nano, the docking port and audio jack are both on the bottom of the unit (see Figure 1-18), and USB 2.0 is the sole method of connection.

Figure 1-18: **The docking port and audio jack are both on the bottom of the second-generation iPod nano.**

How to…

Chapter 2

What's Wrong: Diagnosing Your iPod

Technology breaks, and humans get frustrated. Sometimes you don't know where to start. Sometimes you don't want to know. You just want your stuff to work like it ought to.

Diagnosing your iPod can be a pain, because it isn't always an easy or straightforward task. The meanings of the warning icons and screens might not make a whole lot of sense when they appear and interrupt your tunes. Plus, depending on the circumstances, the same icon might mean different things, from hardware issues to software issues. Who wouldn't get frustrated?

This chapter helps you to sort out what's wrong and take the first steps toward restoring the status quo.

2

1 3 4 5 6 7 8 9 10

NOTE

When you're in the diagnostic menu, the scroll wheel doesn't function. To navigate the menu options, use the Forward and Back buttons instead.

Use the Diagnostic Menu

The diagnostic menu presents a battery of technical tests to run when your iPod is on the fritz. It's invaluable in helping you figure out what's wrong with your iPod, and it's often the first stop on the road to recovery. In this section, we show you how to access the diagnostic menu and navigate its options.

Access the Diagnostic Menu on an Older iPod

To access the diagnostic menu on a first-generation, second-generation, or third-generation iPod:

1. Reset your iPod by holding down the **Menu** and **Play** buttons simultaneously (see Figure 2-1 and Figure 2-2). Don't be too impatient! You need to hold the buttons for five to eight seconds.

Press and hold these together to reset

Figure 2-1: *If you have a first- or second-generation iPod, reset it like this.*

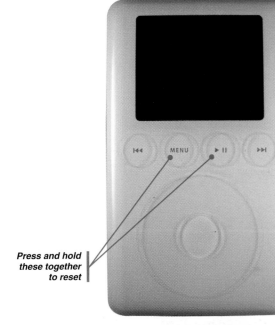

Press and hold
these together
to reset

Figure 2-2: *If you have a third-generation iPod, reset it like this.*

Press and hold
these together
until Apple
logo appears

Figure 2-3: *Hold down the Forward, Back, and Select buttons until the backwards Apple logo appears.*

2. After the iPod shuts down, it should turn back on almost immediately. Once you see the Apple logo appear on the liquid crystal display (LCD), hold down the Forward, Back, and Select buttons simultaneously (see Figure 2-3) until the backwards Apple logo appears. The third-generation iPod makes an audible chirp when you access the diagnostic menu.

3. The next screen asks you to press Play to continue. Press the **Play** button. You can now select options from the diagnostic menu.

Access the Diagnostic Menu on a Newer iPod

To access the diagnostic menu on a fourth- or fifth-generation iPod, an iPod photo, an iPod mini, or an iPod nano:

1. Reset your iPod by holding down the **Menu** and **Select** buttons simultaneously (see Figure 2-4). You need to hold down the buttons for about eight seconds.

Press and hold these together to reset

Figure 2-4: **Hold down the Menu and Select buttons to reset your iPod.**

Press and hold these together until backward Apple logo appear

Figure 2-5: **Hold down the Back and Select buttons until the backwards Apple logo appears.**

2. After the iPod shuts down, it should turn back on almost immediately. Once you see the Apple logo on the LCD, hold down the **Back** and **Select** buttons simultaneously (see Figure 2-5) until the backwards Apple logo appears. You should also hear an audible chirp.

3. The next screen asks you to press Play to continue. Press the **Play** button. You can now select options from the diagnostic menu. If you have an iPod video, press the **Menu** button to run the tests manually, or press the **Previous** button to auto-test the iPod. To see the diagnostic menu, press **Menu**.

OPTION	FUNCTION
5 In 1	Performs multiple tests, including memory, backlight, and the Universal Serial Bus (USB) ports
Reset	Resets the iPod
Key	Checks the keys on the Click Wheel; press a key, and the iPod tells you whether your keypress registered
Chgr Curr	Uncertain, but it appears to turn the charging methods on and off
Remote	Tests the functionality of the remote control; be sure to plug in the remote before running this test
Hp Status	Checks the state of the hold switch and tells you if there is anything plugged into the audio jack
Sleep	Puts the iPod to sleep
Batt A2D	Checks the iPod's power supply
Firewire	Checks the FireWire chip
HDD R/W	Checks that the hard drive can read and write; returns *HDD Pass* if it can
Smrt Dat	Performs another hard drive test
HDD Scan	Scans the hard drive; returns *HDD Pass* or *HDD Fail*, depending on the results of the scan
Read SN	Reads the iPod's serial number
Diskmode	Puts the iPod into Disk Mode
Wheel	Returns different values when you run your thumb around the Click Wheel
Contrast	Checks the contrast of the LCD
Audio	Displays the audio gain
Status	Tells you if you have anything plugged into your iPod
Drv Temp	Displays the temperature of the hard drive
Iram Test	Test the iPod's flash memory

*Table 2-1: **Options in the diagnostic menu***

Decipher the Diagnostic Menu

The diagnostic menu is all about choices, choices, choices, and when you see them, you might feel like you're looking at hieroglyphics. If so, let Table 2-1 be your Rosetta Stone. Not all iPods offer the exact same diagnostic options, so if you don't see some of these in the menu, don't sweat it too much.

To use the diagnostic menu, navigate the options with the Forward and Back buttons, and press the Select button to select an option.

Interpret the Sad Face

When you're in a bad mood, you probably flash a sad face. Your iPod does the same (see Figure 2-6). Its sad face usually appears when there is some sort of hardware issue. For instance, you might see the sad face after you drop your iPod, throw it at someone, or handle it too roughly.

*Figure 2-6: **Your iPod shows a sad face when there is some sort of hardware issue.***

If you're getting the sad face, check your warranty before you do anything else. You should try to get your iPod serviced or replaced under warranty whenever possible. Keep in mind that your warranty won't cover you if Apple determines that you abused your iPod, which is as good a reason as any to treat your property with care.

If your iPod is still under warranty, go with that option. If your warranty has expired, or if you voided the warranty yourself by abusing your iPod, read on.

First, bring up the diagnostic menu as described in "Use the Diagnostic Menu" earlier in this chapter. Scroll down to the HDD Scan option and press the **Select** button to select it. The iPod scans the hard drive, which can take a while to finish.

When the scan is complete, your iPod returns either *HDD Scan Pass* or *HDD Scan Fail*. A failing grade here means that the hard drive is most likely the source of the problem. The good news is that this is something you can fix yourself. We talk about replacing your iPod's hard drive in Chapter 6. The bad news is that you might lose some data, especially if you don't have backup copies of your music files somewhere, like on your computer. You *do* keep backup copies, right?

A passing grade in the hard drive scan means that your hard drive is fine but that your iPod is probably suffering from a bad logic board. You might think that such a repair is way beyond your skill, but actually it's as simple as any other procedure in this book. We show you how to replace the logic board in Chapter 9.

Interpret the Folder Icon

Occasionally, the iPod's folder icon (see Figure 2-7) means the same thing as the sad face—namely, a hardware issue—but more often it means that your iPod is having a software issue. Perhaps your iPod's operating system is not functioning fully or your hard drive is not completely connecting. The chances are pretty good that you can fix your iPod with a minimum of fuss, although you might end up having to replace some parts.

TIP

Always, always, always make backup copies of your data files, including your music files. Your data are more precious than you think. At least one of your authors has learned the true value of data the hard way—by not having adequate backups on hand. Don't be stupid like Marc was. Make backups.

*Figure 2-7: **The iPod's folder icon usually indicates a software issue.***

When you see the folder icon, try resetting the iPod. Hold down the **Menu** and **Play** buttons (first-, second-, and third-generation iPods) or the **Menu** and **Select** buttons (fourth- and fifth-generation iPods, the iPod photo, iPod mini, and iPod nano), and wait about eight seconds. If the folder icon goes away after the iPod restarts, consider the problem solved.

If you're still getting the folder icon, connect the iPod to your computer and try to restore the iPod using iTunes. (See "Troubleshoot Other Problems" later in this chapter for valuable tips about restoring.)

If that doesn't clear up the problem, you might want to check the hard drive connection. To do this, you need to crack open the iPod's case (see Chapter 3 for details). Once you've opened your iPod, disconnect the hard drive connector from the logic board and then plug it back in. Normally, this fix resets the hard drive. It can get the iPod working again—sometimes temporarily, sometimes for the long haul—but you shouldn't attempt it until you're more familiar with the procedures in this book.

Check the Signs of a Low Battery

When John Lennon's energy was on the wane, he wrote tunes like "I'm So Tired" for the Beatles. Your iPod shows icons, screens, and symbols instead.

Nine times out of ten, you can solve all battery issues simply by plugging in, just like Dylan did at the Newport Folk Festival. Occasionally, the battery itself is bad, but now we're getting ahead of ourselves. If your iPod is experiencing power issues, this section gives you a place to start.

Interpret the Low-Battery Icon

The low-battery icon (see Figure 2-8) normally appears when your iPod's charge is low. Older iPods—those with monochrome screens—show this icon. When you see it, connect your iPod to your computer or plug it into a wall charger. If charging doesn't take care of the problem, you might need a new battery.

TIP

For best results, always charge your iPod's battery with a wall charger instead of via USB or FireWire. Sometimes when the charge is low, your iPod doesn't have enough juice to run its data ports! If the data ports aren't working reliably, you can't use them to draw a charge.

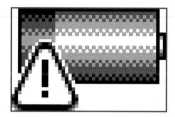

Figure 2-8: **The low-battery icon appears when your older iPod's charge is low.**

Assuming regular use, an iPod battery lasts about a year to a year and a half. Most iPod batteries are rated at 500 full-charge cycles—that's 500 recharges after depleting your battery completely. But you probably charge your battery while it still has some kick, so those 500 full charges work out to about 1,000 to 2,000 partial charges, depending on how much of the charge you tend to use up.

If you keep seeing the low-battery icon, or if the charge in your battery doesn't last as long as it once did, you should get a new battery for your iPod. We talk about replacing the battery in Chapter 4.

If you get the low-battery icon while your iPod is plugged into the charger, your charger might be bad and you should think about replacing it. You should always go with an Original Equipment Manufacturer (OEM) charger or one made specifically for the iPod by Apple. Brandon can't recommend the aftermarket stuff; it's too unreliable, and it might even fry your iPod's insides.

Interpret the Low-Battery Warning Screen

The low-battery warning screen (see Figure 2-9) is the new version of the low-battery icon. It displays on all the newer iPods—the ones with a color display, that is—when the iPod's charge is low.

Low Battery
No battery power remains. Please connect iPod to power.

Figure 2-9: **On color iPods, you get the low-battery warning screen when the charge is low.**

When you see this warning screen, follow the same steps we outlined in "Interpret the Low-Battery Icon"—namely, hook up the iPod to your computer or plug it into a charger.

Interpret the Low-Battery Symbol

On some iPods, when the battery is fully (or nearly fully) depleted and you try to connect to a computer through USB, the low-battery symbol appears (see Figure 2-10). Normally, when you see this symbol, you can just leave the iPod connected, and it will eventually charge. Sometimes, the iPod doesn't charge, however, and the low-battery symbol doesn't go away. If this happens to you, purchase a wall charger for your iPod. You might also try leaving your iPod on for 24 hours to deplete the battery completely and then plug the iPod into the computer.

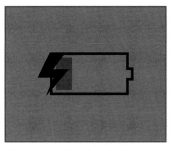

Figure 2-10: **The low-battery symbol on certain iPods appears when the battery is fully depleted.**

Troubleshoot Other Problems

Your iPod is a complex little bugger, and a lot can go wrong with it. In this section, we look at some additional icons and warning signs, and show you how to fix them.

QUICKSTEPS

DETERMINING YOUR iPOD'S SOFTWARE VERSION

Your iPod comes with a sophisticated software operating system, just like your computer does. To see what version of software your iPod is running:

1. Press the **Menu** button.

2. Scroll down to the **Settings** selection.

3. Find and select the **About** menu.

You'll note that you used the About menu in Chapter 1 to determine your iPod's storage capacity.

TIP

Make sure all your music is fully backed up to iTunes before attempting to restore your iPod. Otherwise, you will lose your data. You don't want that kind of hassle. Just ask Marc.

Interpret the Use iTunes To Restore Screen

"Connect to your computer. Use iTunes to restore." Ever come across this screen? It appears when your iPod is experiencing certain kinds of software issues. Not all iPods show this warning. You see it on fifth-generation iPods with software version 1.1.2 or later, first-generation iPod nanos with software version 1.2 or later, and all second-generation iPod nanos.

At the risk of stating the obvious, when you see this screen, you need to restore your iPod. *Restoring* the iPod means wiping the disk drive completely clean and reloading the original factory settings. It's the iPod equivalent of a total system restore on your computer. You complete this procedure through the iTunes software, not through your iPod's diagnostic menu.

To start, simply connect your iPod to your computer and follow the prompts.

On a Mac, you see a message in iTunes that says, "The software on the iPod 'My iPod' is damaged and needs to be repaired before it can be used with iTunes. Would you like to repair your iPod software now?" Click OK to proceed.

On a Windows PC, a message pops up that says, "iPod Not Readable. This iPod needs to be reformatted for use on your PC. Click on the Update button below to run the application that will allow you to reformat or restore your iPod." Just click Update to proceed.

Handle a Frozen Apple Logo

Normally, when you turn on your iPod, the Apple logo appears for a couple of seconds before the iPod loads to the main menu. Occasionally, the iPod gets stuck on this logo.

If this happens to you, put the iPod into Disk Mode through the diagnostic menu. Then connect the iPod to your computer and update or restore the iPod. Sometimes you can get away with just updating the iPod, so try that first, but usually you have to restore the iPod, too. As before, make backups of your music files, because the restore procedure will obliterate them.

Interpret the Power Icon

Once your iPod has been restored on your computer, you might receive a prompt to plug your iPod into an external power supply. If so, when you disconnect the iPod from the computer, the power icon appears. This isn't exactly an error; it's perfectly normal and expected, although you need to deal with it before you can use your iPod again.

To make the power icon go away, just plug the iPod into an external power supply. You then see the Apple logo with a progress bar underneath it. Just a little longer now! When your iPod finishes the operation, it should be back to working normally.

Chapter 3
Cracking the Case

Opening your iPod might seem like breaking into the music industry (as in impossible without the right connections), but it really isn't as bad as all that. In fact, with the right tools and the right state of mind, this is one tough nut that's easy to crack.

In this chapter, we show you how to open your iPod. You should read this chapter before proceeding with any other repair in this book. Do yourself a favor, too, and read the instructions for your iPod all the way through before you get down to business. That's just basic orienteering. If you know where you're going beforehand, you minimize your chances of getting lost.

Gather the Tools

Believe it or not, there are actually commercially available tools specifically designed for opening iPods, as shown in the illustration on the next page.

These tools are made from plastic, which helps to prevent you from scratching your iPod's case, and they're relatively inexpensive as far as tools go, as in about ten clams U.S. Finding them takes a bit of diligence. Any place that sells iPod batteries probably also stocks these tools. You can always get them on Brandon's Web site, www.synctogo.com, or you might try your luck on eBay. In any event, they're your best choice for opening the case, but they're not absolutely essential. In a pinch, you can substitute tools that you probably already have in your toolbox, but do try to get the plastic ones.

In lieu of the plastic tools, go for a small, optical, flat-headed screwdriver—the smaller the better.

If you're in need of one of these, Brandon has you covered on www.synctogo.com, or you can go to the local hardware store. When you use the screwdriver instead of the plastic tools, you want to be careful. Don't apply too much force, or you might damage your iPod. The chances are good that you will at least scratch your iPod no matter how gently you go with the screwdriver, so make a point of finding those plastic tools.

For the first-, second-, third-, and fourth-generation iPod, as well as the iPod photo, if you need to replace the screen (see Chapter 5), the front panel (see Chapter 8), or the logic board (see Chapter 9), you need a T6 Torx screwdriver.

GET READY FOR REPAIR WORK, OR ZEN AND THE ART OF iPOD MAINTENANCE

You have the tools. You have this book. But do you have the most important element for any repair job? That's right—we're talking about your mental game. How's it going in there? Are you calm and focused or frazzled and distracted? And what's the current status of your environment?

You wouldn't attempt to repair your iPod with both hands tied behind your back for obvious reasons. Perhaps less obviously but for the very same reasons, you shouldn't attempt to repair your iPod without giving it your full attention. Try to set aside a block of you-time for the job, without the usual million interruptions that come with day-to-day life. Don't attempt to squeeze in your repair between band practice and baseball over a burrito. Sequester yourself in a room, maybe. Turn off the cell phone. Turn off the TV. Take a couple of deep breaths; it can't hurt, and it works wonders for ninjas.

The place that you choose to repair your iPod feeds back into your mental game, so choose wisely, grasshopper. You want good lighting so that you can see what you're doing. If the available lighting isn't cutting it, borrow your desk lamp or another portable source.

You also want a clean, flat surface to work on. You don't need the whole kitchen table, for example, but you do need more space than the typical cramped computer station. You'll be working with electronic components, so avoid excessive dust and static electricity. In fact, doing a little dusting beforehand is smart, because it gives you a chance to depressurize and ratchet up your mental game.

Continued . . .

This is a specialty item that you might not have on hand unless you fix cell phones. If you're lucky, your local hardware store stocks them. If not, you can find one online without too much trouble.

If you're repairing an iPod mini or a second-generation iPod nano, you should round up a small Phillips-head screwdriver. This is in addition to the flat-headed screwdriver or the plastic tools.

Also, with regards to opening the iPod mini and the second-generation iPod nano, consider grabbing your hair dryer. You can use a heat gun if you like, but sometimes the gun gets too hot and melts parts of the iPod—not good. Also, most people have hair dryers lying around, while heat guns are less common. Now, a word of advice: A heat source isn't absolutely necessary here. You can usually get away without using one, and because you can end up doing serious damage to your iPod, you have ample reason for pause. At the same time, you might find it easier to open your iPod mini or second-generation iPod nano if you apply a little heat, so weigh the pros and the cons, and decide for yourself.

Open Your iPod

Some iPods love to pop right open, while some just want to stay closed, but patience rewards all practitioners. Keep at it, and don't get too frustrated; anyone can open any iPod. (The same holds true as dating advice.) We talk about the iPod mini and the iPod nano later in this chapter.

Open Your First- or Second-Generation iPod

To open a first- or second-generation iPod:

1. Turn the iPod on its side, and measure about two inches from the bottom.
2. Take your plastic tool or flat-headed screwdriver, and carefully but firmly wedge it between the plastic front and the metal back at the position you located in step 1. If you have problems, you might try running your tool along the crack and gradually working it in.

GET READY FOR REPAIR WORK, OR ZEN AND THE ART OF iPOD MAINTENANCE *(Continued)*

You also might consider draping a soft cloth over your workspace or working on an oversized mouse pad. This way, you minimize the distance that small parts will roll.

Then get yourself into a comfortable chair or stool that allows you to move your arms and hands freely. Straighten that back of yours, and put those feet flat on the ground. Take another deep ninja breath, and you're good to go.

As you work, you might want to keep a digital camera handy and snap a quick photo of each stage of your repair job. If you get lost, or if you forget exactly where a part should go, you can refer back to your photo log and clear up the issue.

NOTE

All the step-by-step instructions in this section start off with you measuring two inches from the bottom of your iPod. This is where you'll insert your plastic tool or flat-headed screwdriver. While you can open your iPod from a different spot, two inches from the bottom is the easiest and best location in Brandon's experience.

TIP

On a first- or second-generation iPod, the back can get hung up around the audio jack and the hold switch, so be careful as you remove it. Also, on a second-generation iPod, sometimes the battery sticks to the back. Gently unstick the battery before you pull the back all the way off.

3. Use the plastic tool or the flat-headed screwdriver as a lever to crack open the case (see Figure 3-1).

*Figure 3-1: **Crack open the case.***

4. Carefully slide the plastic tool or the flat-headed screwdriver down the side of the iPod to release all the clips that hold it together (see Figure 3-2).

*Figure 3-2: **Release the clips.***

5. Carefully remove the back from the iPod (see Figure 3-3).

*Figure 3-3: **Remove the back.***

Open Your Third- or Fourth-Generation iPod or Your iPod Photo

To open a third- or fourth-generation iPod or an iPod photo:

1. Turn the iPod on its side, and measure about two inches from the bottom.

2. Take your plastic tool or flat-headed screwdriver, and carefully but firmly wedge it between the plastic front and the metal back at the position you located in step 1.

3. Use the plastic tool or the flat-headed screwdriver as a lever to crack open the case.

4. Carefully slide the plastic tool or the flat-headed screwdriver down the side of the iPod to release all the clips that hold it together.

5. Begin to remove the back from the iPod, but don't take it all the way off just yet. As soon as you can, unplug the audio jack (see Figure 3-4). Do this before completely taking off the back. If you don't, you can damage your iPod. To unplug the audio jack, try using your fingers, or pry the audio jack with your opening tool if the jack won't budge. The audio cable attached to the jack is delicate, so easy does it.

*Figure 3-4: **Unplug the audio jack.***

7. With the audio jack unplugged, take the back the rest of the way off.

Open Your iPod Video

To open your fifth-generation iPod:

1. Turn the iPod on its side, and measure about two inches from the bottom of the unit.

2. Take your plastic tool or flat-headed screwdriver, and carefully but firmly wedge it between the plastic front and the metal back at the position you located in step 1.

3. Use the plastic tool or the flat-headed screwdriver as a lever to crack open the case.

4. Carefully slide the plastic tool or the flat-headed screwdriver down the side of the iPod to release all the clips that hold it together.

5. Gently pick up the back, but don't take it all the way off just yet. Notice that there are two ribbon cables connecting the back to the logic board of the iPod (see Figure 3-5).

*Figure 3-5: **Reveal the ribbon cables.***

6. Unplug the cables from the logic board one at a time (see Figure 3-6). The connectors are held with a clip. Release the clip, and pull the cables out. Be very gentle with the cables; they can tear rather easily.

7. With the cables unplugged, take the back the rest of the way off (see Figure 3-7).

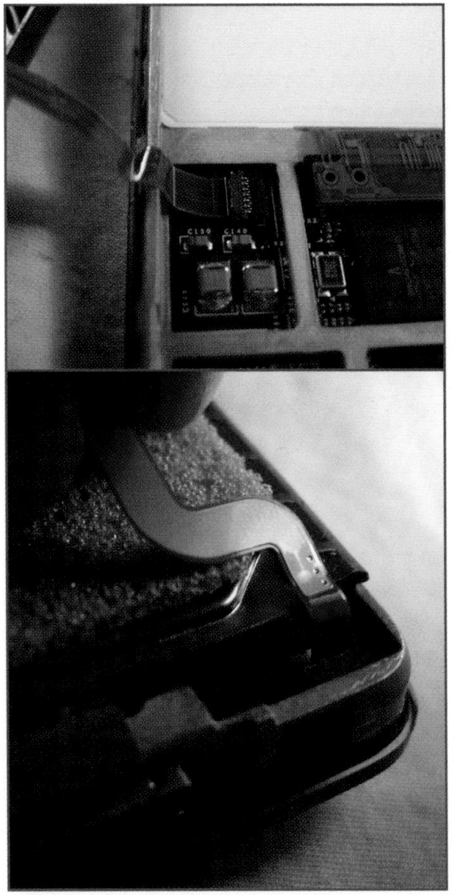

*Figure 3-7: **Remove the back.***

*Figure 3-6: **Unplug the ribbon cables.***

Open Your iPod Mini

To open a first- or second-generation iPod mini:

1. This step is optional, so feel free to skip it. With your hair dryer or heat gun, heat the top and bottom pieces of the iPod mini until they are fairly warm to the touch. Your goal here is to soften up the adhesive behind the plastic. You do *not* want to deform the plastic or melt it.

2. Carefully pry off the white plastic pieces on the top and bottom of the iPod mini. To do this, wedge your plastic tool or flat-headed screwdriver between the metal shell and the white plastic pieces (see Figure 3-8).

Figure 3-8: *Pry off the plastic pieces.*

3. At the top of the iPod mini, you see two small screws: one on each side (see Figure 3-9). With your Phillips-head screwdriver, remove both screws.

Figure 3-9: *Remove the screws on the top.*

4. At the bottom of the iPod mini, you see a small piece of metal. You need to remove it, but don't worry. It should come out easily enough. The piece of metal is spring-clipped in place. Dislodge the two clips; a screwdriver works better here than your

*Figure 3-10: **Pry out the piece of metal on the bottom.***

plastic tool. Then pry out the piece of metal with your plastic tool or flat-headed screwdriver (see Figure 3-10).

*Figure 3-11: **Unplug the Click Wheel connector.***

*Figure 3-12: **Slide out the insides.***

5. Behind the piece of metal, you see the button of the Click Wheel. Gently—for the love of Janis, gently—unplug the Click Wheel connector (see Figure 3-11).

6. Carefully push from the bottom, and slide the insides of the iPod mini out through the top (see Figure 3-12) as you hum "Within You Without You" from *Sgt. Pepper.*

Open Your iPod Nano

How you go about opening an iPod nano depends on the generation. First-generation iPod nanos go much like the regular iPod, while second-generation iPod nanos are much like the iPod mini, as this section shows.

Open Your First-Generation iPod Nano

To open a first-generation iPod nano:

1. Turn the iPod nano on its side, and measure about two inches from the bottom of the unit.
2. Take your plastic tool or flat-headed screwdriver, and carefully but firmly wedge it into the side of the iPod nano at the position you located in step 1.
3. Use the plastic tool or the flat-headed screwdriver as a lever to crack open the case.
4. Carefully slide the plastic tool or the flat-headed screwdriver down the side of the iPod nano to release all the clips that hold it together.
5. Remove the back from the iPod nano (see Figure 3-13).

*Figure 3-13: **Remove the back.***

Open a Second-Generation iPod Nano

To open a second-generation iPod nano:

1. This step is optional, so feel free to skip it. With your hair dryer or heat gun, heat the top and bottom pieces of the iPod nano until they are fairly warm to the touch. As with the iPod mini, you want to soften up the adhesive that holds the plastic, not deform the plastic or melt it.

2. Carefully pry off the plastic pieces on the top and bottom of the iPod nano by wedging your plastic tool or flat-headed screwdriver between the metal shell and the plastic pieces.

3. At the top of the iPod nano, you see two small screws, one on each side (see Figure 3-14). With your Phillips-head screwdriver, remove both screws.

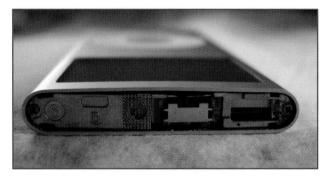

Figure 3-14: Remove the screws on the top.

4. At the bottom of the iPod nano, you see two more small screws (see Figure 3-15). With your Phillips-head screwdriver, remove those as well.

Figure 3-15: Remove the screws on the bottom.

TIP

Sometimes you can heat the plastic pieces sufficiently by pressing the iPod nano between your hands.

5. Pull out the audio jack, but don't pull it all the way out, because it is attached by a ribbon cable (see Figure 3-16). Handle both the jack and the cable carefully.

*Figure 3-16: **Pull out the audio jack.***

6. Under the audio jack, you find another screw that was previously hidden. Take out this screw as well (see Figure 3-17).

*Figure 3-17: **Remove the screw under the audio jack.***

QUICKSTEPS

PUT YOUR iPOD BACK TOGETHER

All the king's horses and all the king's men couldn't do diddley for Humpty Dumpty, but your iPod isn't a large, anthropomorphic egg, so you don't need to call out the cavalry.

To close the case back up when you're done making your repairs, simply run the instructions for opening the case in reverse.

7. Take out the small metal bracket that surrounds the docking port by prying it gently with your plastic tool or flat-headed screwdriver (see Figure 3-18).

*Figure 3-18: **Remove the small metal bracket.***

8. Disconnect the audio jack from the logic board. (This step can be a little sketchy, because you can't completely see what you're doing.) To do this, take your plastic tool or flat-headed screwdriver, and carefully pull the audio-jack connector toward the front of the iPod until the connector comes unplugged (see Figure 3-19). However, do not remove the audio jack from the iPod, as it is still connected to the Click Wheel.

*Figure 3-19: **Disconnect the audio jack from the logic board.***

9. Very carefully take your plastic tool or flat-headed screwdriver, and push the logic board through the casing (see Figure 3-20). Note that the Click Wheel and audio jack remain *inside* the casing.

Figure 3-20: *Slide the logic board through the casing.*

Chapter 4

Power Issues: Replacing Your Battery and Other Power Concerns

With a little luck, your most pressing power concerns these days are reducing your carbon shoe size and hoping that they don't re-form Power Station. If you're experiencing additional power troubles—for example, with regards to your iPod— perhaps this chapter can be of service.

Whenever the words *iPod* and *power* come up in the same sentence, Brandon immediately thinks of the battery. Replacing iPod batteries is one of the most common repairs that his company Synctogo.com makes, because, over time, the battery is the component most likely to fail.

As far as repairs go, replacing the battery isn't especially technical. In fact, for most iPods, it's probably the easiest

repair in this entire book, although, as you'll see, the going gets tougher with the iPod mini and the iPod nano.

Occasionally, the battery isn't the source of your power trouble. We conclude this chapter with suggestions and advice for dealing with non-battery power concerns.

Check the Signs of a Bad Battery

What makes a battery go bad? A troubled home environment? Actually, it's not so sad a story. Your battery goes bad naturally just from regular use. It has a lifetime of about a year to a year and a half, or about 500 full-charge cycles. After that, it starts to show its age.

The most common sign that your battery is ready to be replaced is that it doesn't hold a charge for as long as it once did. You find yourself plugging in your iPod more regularly, and the battery seems to get depleted more quickly.

Another sure sign is that the low-battery warning appears constantly on your iPod's liquid crystal display (LCD). Whether you get an icon or a warning screen depends on your model of iPod. See Chapter 2 for details.

You might also find that your iPod works fine when you plug it into a charger, but that it dies immediately when you attempt to run it from the battery. In this case, your battery isn't just dying; it's dead. Time for a replacement.

Replace the Battery in Your iPod

Table 4-1 shows the required tools and the difficulty level for replacing the battery in an iPod. We talk about the iPod mini and the iPod nano in subsequent sections in this chapter.

iPOD MODEL	TOOLS NEEDED	DIFFICULTY LEVEL
First-generation iPod	iPod-opening tools or flat-headed screwdriver	Easy
Second-generation iPod	iPod-opening tools or flat-headed screwdriver	Easy
Third-generation iPod	iPod-opening tools or flat-headed screwdriver	Easy
Fourth-generation iPod (monochrome)	iPod-opening tools or flat-headed screwdriver	Easy
iPod photo (fourth-generation color iPod)	iPod-opening tools or flat-headed screwdriver	Easy
iPod video (fifth-generation iPod)	iPod-opening tools or flat-headed screwdriver	Moderate

Table 4-1: Tools Needed and Difficulty Level of Replacing the Battery in an iPod

Replace the Battery in a First- or Second-Generation iPod

To replace the battery in a first- or second-generation iPod:

1. Open the iPod according to the instructions in Chapter 3.
2. Unplug the battery from the logic board (see Figure 4-1).

Figure 4-1: Unplug the battery from the logic board.

3. Pull the battery from the iPod (see Figure 4-2). A small piece of adhesive holds the battery in place, so you might need to apply a little force.

4. Plug the new battery into the logic board (see Figure 4-3).

Figure 4-2: Remove the battery from the iPod.

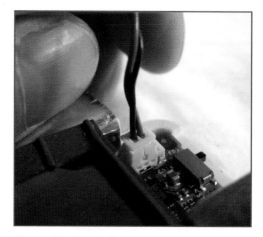

Figure 4-3: Plug in the new battery.

5. Put the new battery where the old one was, exactly as it was (see Figure 4-4).

6. Put the iPod back together.

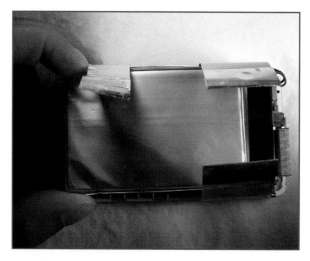

Figure 4-4: Put the new battery into place.

Replace the Battery in a Third-Generation iPod

To replace the battery in a third-generation iPod:

1. Open the iPod according to the instructions in Chapter 3.

2. Disconnect the audio jack (see Figure 4-5). If you don't disconnect the audio jack, you will have problems.

3. Slide the hard drive from the hard drive connector (see Figure 4-6).

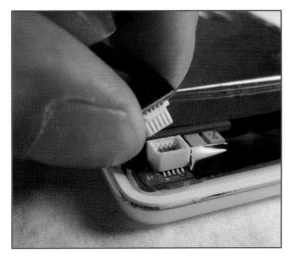

Figure 4-5: Disconnect the audio jack.

Figure 4-6: Remove the hard drive.

4. Unplug the hard drive connector from the logic board (see Figure 4-7).

*Figure 4-7: Disconnect the
hard drive connector.*

5. Unplug the battery from the logic board (see Figure 4-8).

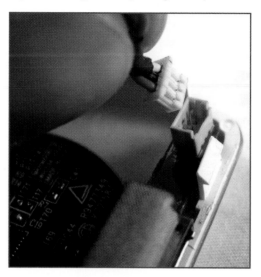

Figure 4-8: Unplug the battery.

6. Remove the battery from the iPod (see Figure 4-9).

Figure 4-9: Remove the battery.

7. Put the new battery where the old one was, exactly as it was (see Figure 4-10).

Figure 4-10: Put the new battery into place.

8. Plug the new battery into the logic board (see Figure 4-11).

Figure 4-11: Plug in the new battery.

9. Plug the hard drive connector back into the logic board (see Figure 4-12).

10. Slide the hard drive into the hard drive connector (see Figure 4-13).

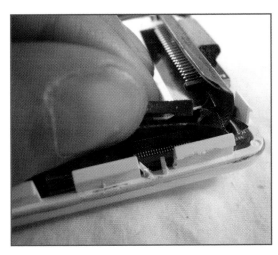

Figure 4-12: Plug in the hard drive connector.

Figure 4-13: Slide the hard drive back in.

Figure 4-14: Plug in the audio jack.

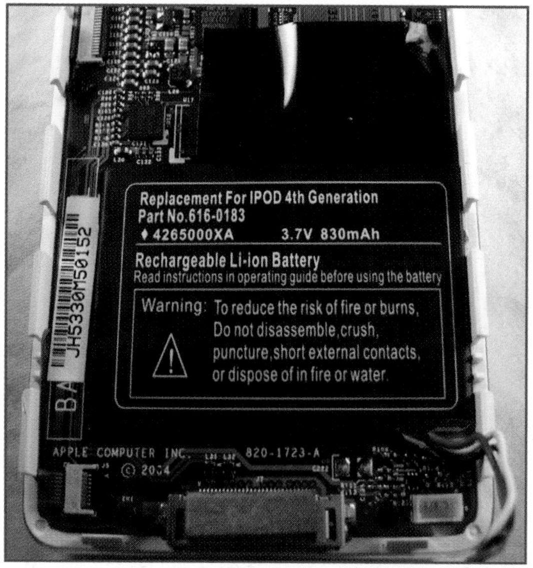

Figure 4-16: Put the new battery in the iPod.

11. Plug the audio jack back into the logic board (see Figure 4-14).

12. Put the iPod back together.

Replace the Battery in a Fourth-Generation iPod or an iPod Photo

To replace the battery in a fourth-generation iPod or an iPod photo:

1. Open your iPod according to the instructions in Chapter 3.

2. Disconnect the audio jack from the logic board.

3. Carefully slide the hard drive from the hard drive connector.

4. Unplug the battery.

5. Carefully remove the battery from the iPod (see Figure 4-15). The battery is glued down with some adhesive; you will most likely need to pry it out with your plastic opening tool or flat-headed screwdriver.

Figure 4-15: Remove the battery.

6. Place the new battery in the iPod (see Figure 4-16).

7. Reconnect the battery cable, and make sure to tuck it away properly. Normally, you place the cable under the logic board.

8. Slide the hard drive back into the hard drive connector. Make sure that the hard drive is fully connected; you don't want a loose connection.

9. Plug the audio jack back into the logic board (see Figure 4-17).

10. Put the iPod back together.

*Figure 4-17: **Reconnect the audio jack.***

Replace the Battery in an iPod Video

To replace the battery in a fifth-generation iPod:

1. Open your iPod according to the instructions in Chapter 3.

2. Disconnect the battery from its connector (see Figure 4-18). Notice the small clip; carefully pull it up.

*Figure 4-18: **Unplug the battery.***

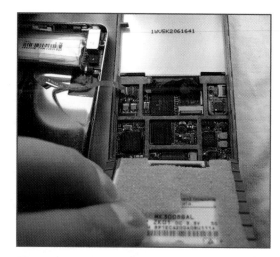

Figure 4-19: Lift up the hard drive.

3. Carefully lift up the hard drive (see Figure 4-19).

4. Still holding the hard drive, unclip the audio jack from the logic board (see Figure 4-20).

Figure 4-20: Release the audio jack.

5. Carefully pry the battery from the back of the iPod (see Figure 4-21). The battery is glued into place.

6. Place the new battery on the back of the iPod (see Figure 4-22).

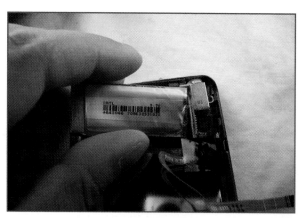

Figure 4-21: Pry off the battery.

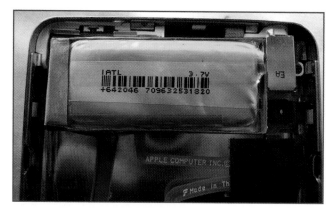

Figure 4-22: Place the new battery.

7. Plug the audio jack back into the logic board (see Figure 4-23).

8. Plug the new battery into the logic board (see Figure 4-24).

9. Put the iPod back together.

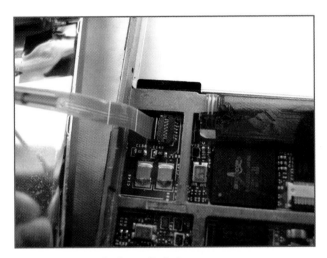

Figure 4-23: Plug in the audio jack.

Figure 4-24: Plug in the new battery.

Replace the Battery in Your iPod Mini

A bad battery in an iPod mini poses a bit more of a challenge (see Table 4-2), but don't let that deter you. You have our full confidence. You can succeed in this task.

iPOD MINI MODEL	TOOLS NEEDED	DIFFICULTY LEVEL
First-generation iPod mini	iPod-opening tools, small Phillips-head screwdriver, flat-headed screwdriver	Moderate
Second-generation iPod mini	iPod-opening tools, small Phillips-head screwdriver, flat-headed screwdriver	Moderate

Table 4-2: Tools Needed and Difficulty Level of Replacing the Battery in an iPod Mini

To replace the battery in either generation of iPod mini:

1. Open the iPod mini, and slide out the logic board according to the directions in Chapter 3.

2. Locate the battery (see Figure 4-25).

Figure 4-25: **Here is the battery in the iPod mini.**

3. Unplug the battery from the logic board (see Figure 4-26).

Figure 4-26: **Unplug the battery.**

Figure 4-27: Remove the battery.

4. Remove the old battery from the logic board (see Figure 4-27).

5. Place the new battery into the iPod mini.

6. Connect the new battery to the logic board.

7. Slide the logic board back into the mini's shell (see Figure 4-28).

Figure 4-28: Slide the logic board back in.

8. Put the iPod mini back together. Replace the screws in the top, put the metal clip back in the bottom, and place the plastic pieces on the top and the bottom, just as you found them. There should be enough adhesive to attach these pieces. If not, try a little rubber cement.

Replace the Battery in Your First-Generation iPod Nano

The iPod nano is super-small, which makes replacing its battery something of a test for the non-repair professional—not only because of the size, but also because you need to solder the battery to the logic board (see Table 4-3). If you don't have access to a soldering iron, or if the idea of soldering your iPod nano doesn't exactly fill you with confidence, you might be better off leaving this one to the pros.

iPOD NANO MODEL	TOOLS NEEDED	DIFFICULTY LEVEL
First-generation iPod nano	iPod-opening tools, soldering iron, solder	Hard
Second-generation iPod nano	Not advised	Do not attempt

Table 4-3: Tools Needed and Difficulty Level of Replacing the Battery in an iPod Nano

In this section, we give step-by-step instructions for replacing the battery in your first-generation iPod nano. We don't even touch replacing the battery in the second-generation nano, because the steps are too hard for a non-pro, and if you make a mistake, you can easily do permanent damage to your iPod. Also, don't try to use the procedure for the first-generation nano for replacing the battery in a second-generation nano, because the steps aren't the same. Find yourself an iPod repair service instead.

To replace the battery in a first-generation iPod nano:

1. Open your iPod nano according to the instructions in Chapter 3.

2. Locate the battery (see Figure 4-29). It's soldered to the logic board.

3. Carefully remove the battery from the logic board (see Figure 4-30). You will need to pull the wires off.

Figure 4-29: The battery in an iPod nano is soldered to the logic board.

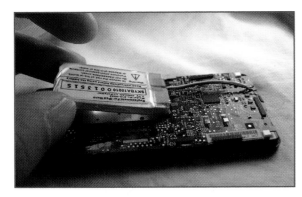

Figure 4-30: Remove the battery.

4. With your soldering iron, solder the new battery onto the logic board (see Figure 4-31).

5. Put the iPod nano back together.

Figure 4-31: Solder the new battery onto the logic board.

Still No Power? Try These Fixes

Always install a new battery first to resolve any iPod power issues. If the new battery doesn't seem to do the trick, then you might try the following:

- Double-check all the connections for the new battery. Sometimes a wire can come loose, or it might be pinched. If so, your iPod might not be able to power on.
- If all the connections are good, try charging your iPod overnight through the wall charger.
- If that doesn't work, try a new charger.
- If that doesn't work, try restoring your iPod with the latest iPod software through iTunes. See Chapter 2 for more information about restoring.

If you've tried all these suggestions and you are still experiencing power problems—your iPod isn't holding a good charge, or your iPod isn't powering on even when you plug it into a charger—then most likely a bad logic board is the culprit. See Chapter 9 for how to replace it.

If the battery icon goes away but you start getting different icons or warning messages, see Chapter 2 for information on interpreting the icons.

Chapter 5

Can't See a Thing: Replacing Broken Screens

Remember when Kilroy flipped the switch on his laser video and saw Dr. Righteous staring back at him? Obviously, the screen on his laser video was working just fine. Hopefully, you can say the same for the screen on your iPod, but if you can't, this chapter is for you. In it, we show you how to remove your iPod's broken liquid crystal display (LCD) and install a brand-new one.

Check the Signs of a Bad Screen

A bad screen is fairly easy to diagnose. When you turn on your iPod, you see what looks like an inkblot in the display. Sometimes it seems to be a large crack or a flood of ink, while other times it looks more like a little sliver (see Figure 5-1).

Either way, your LCD needs to be replaced. You don't break open the screen itself and try to clean up the spilled ink. You just pop out the old screen and install a new one.

Figure 5-1: *A broken LCD looks something like this.*

Replace Your iPod's Screen

Table 5-1 shows the required tools and the difficulty level of replacing the screen on an iPod. We discuss the iPod mini and the iPod nano later on in this chapter.

iPOD MODEL	TOOLS NEEDED	DIFFICULTY LEVEL
First-generation iPod	iPod-opening tools or flat-headed screwdriver and T6 Torx screwdriver	Moderate
Second-generation iPod	iPod-opening tools or flat-headed screwdriver and T6 Torx screwdriver	Moderate
Third-generation iPod	iPod-opening tools or flat-headed screwdriver and T6 Torx screwdriver	Moderate
Fourth-generation iPod (monochrome)	iPod-opening tools or flat-headed screwdriver and T6 Torx screwdriver	Moderate
iPod photo (fourth-generation color iPod)	iPod-opening tools or flat-headed screwdriver and T6 Torx screwdriver	Moderate
iPod video (fifth-generation iPod)	iPod-opening tools or flat-headed screwdriver and Phillips-head screwdriver	Hard

Table 5-1: *Tools Needed and Difficulty Level of Replacing the Screen in an iPod*

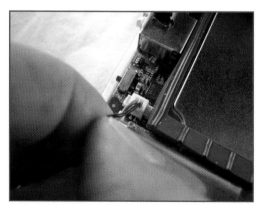

Figure 5-2: *Pull the battery from the hard drive.*

Figure 5-3: *Unplug the battery.*

Replace the Screen in a First-Generation iPod

To replace the screen in a first-generation iPod:

1. Open the iPod according to the instructions in Chapter 3.

2. Pull the battery from the back of the hard drive (see Figure 5-2). There is adhesive holding it down.

3. Unplug the battery from the logic board (see Figure 5-3).

4. Carefully slide the hard drive from the orange hard drive connector.

Kilroy Was Here, the 1983 concept album from American pseudo-progressive quasi-rockers Styx, tells the story of a world gone wrong, where self-righteous ideologues enjoy absolute rule, pseudo-progressive quasi-rock stars are imprisoned for exercising their First Amendment rights, and androids called *robotos* handle all the blue-collar jobs. It sold millions of copies. (And it was the first album that Marc ever bought. Hey, he was 12.) The first single from the album, the inimitable "Mr. Roboto," awash in synthesizers and light disco stylings, occupies a strange place in pop music history, as it will never be forgotten despite its near-total lack of musical content.

QUICKFACTS

GET AND TROUBLESHOOT A NEW SCREEN

Your best bet for acquiring a new screen for your iPod is to do an Internet search. To save yourself a little time and effort, Brandon sells replacement screens at www.Synctogo.com. You might also check eBay for bargains.

The cost of a new screen varies widely, depending on the iPod model and the supplier. You'll pay anywhere from $30 to $100 U.S. Monochrome screens for older iPods are generally less expensive than the color displays for later models.

Sometimes, after you install a new screen, the display appears grainy. Just reset your iPod, and this problem should clear right up.

5. Pull the hard drive from the iPod (see Figure 5-4).

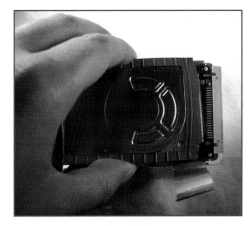

Figure 5-4: *Pull out the hard drive.*

6. Find the four T6 Torx screws in the logic board. A large piece of rubber covers one of them; remove the rubber to expose the fourth screw (see Figure 5-5).

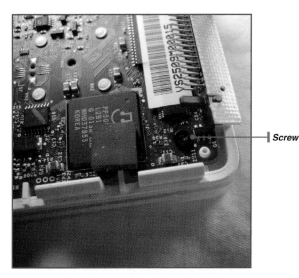

Screw

Figure 5-5: *Remove the piece of rubber to expose the fourth T6 Torx screw.*

Figure 5-7: Remove the logic board.

7. With your T6 Torx screwdriver, remove all four screws (see Figure 5-6).

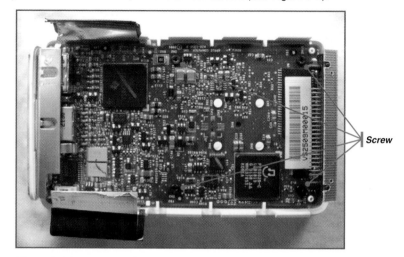

Screw

Figure 5-6: Remove the T6 Torx screws.

8. Remove the logic board from the bottom of the iPod (see Figure 5-7).

9. The screen has four white clips: two on each side of the logic board. These clips hold the screen in place. Disconnect them (see Figure 5-8).

Figure 5-8: Unclip the screen.

10. Find the connector for the screen underneath the scroll wheel. Carefully unplug this connector with your iPod-opening tool or small flat-headed screwdriver (see Figure 5-9).

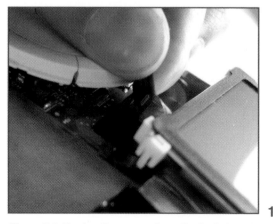

Figure 5-9: Unplug the screen from the logic board.

11. Connect the new screen to the logic board.

12. Connect the four white clips, and make sure they're holding the screen in place.

13. Screw in all four T6 Torx screws to the logic board.

14. Slide the hard drive back into the hard drive connector.

15. Plug the battery back into the logic board.

16. Put the iPod back together.

Replace the Screen in a Second-Generation iPod

To replace the screen in a second-generation iPod:

1. Open the iPod according to the instructions in Chapter 3.

2. Pull the battery from the back of the hard drive. There is adhesive holding it down.

3. Unplug the battery from the logic board.

4. Carefully slide the hard drive from the orange hard drive connector.

5. Notice the two small brown clips next to the hard drive connector. Pull down on them to loosen the connector, and remove it from the logic board (see Figure 5-10).

6. Pull the blue piece of rubber from the iPod (see Figure 5-11).

*Figure 5-10: **Remove the hard drive connector.***

*Figure 5-11: **Pull out the piece of rubber.***

7. Loosen the scroll wheel's connector by pulling down on the brown tabs, just like you did with the hard drive connector in step 5 (see Figure 5-12).

*Figure 5-12: **Loosen the scroll wheel's connector.***

8. Remove all eight T6 Torx screws from the logic board (see Figure 5-13).

Screw

*Figure 5-13: **Remove the T6 Torx screws.***

Figure 5-14: *Release the scroll wheel's connector.*

9. Carefully lift the logic board enough to release the scroll wheel's connector (see Figure 5-14).

10. Remove the logic board (see Figure 5-15).

Figure 5-15: *Remove the logic board.*

11. Release the white side clips holding the screen to the logic board (see Figure 5-16).

Figure 5-16: *Unclip the screen.*

12. Carefully unplug the connector holding the screen to the logic board (see Figure 5-17).

*Figure 5-17: **Unplug the screen from the logic board.***

13. Connect the new screen.

14. Place the logic board back in the iPod, and screw in all eight T6 Torx screws.

15. Plug in the scroll wheel's ribbon cable.

16. Reattach the hard drive connector, and replace the blue piece of rubber.

17. Slide the hard drive into place.

18. Plug the battery into the logic board, and place the battery on top of the hard drive.

19. Put the iPod back together.

Replace the Screen in a Third-Generation iPod

To replace the screen in a third-generation iPod:

1. Open the iPod according to the instructions in Chapter 3.

2. Unplug the audio jack from the logic board (see Figure 5-18).

3. Slide the hard drive from the hard drive connector, and remove the hard drive from the iPod (see Figure 5-19).

*Figure 5-18: **Unplug the audio jack.***

Figure 5-19: **Remove the hard drive.**

4. Unplug the hard drive connector from the logic board, and remove it from the iPod (see Figure 5-20).

Plug

Connector

Figure 5-20: **Remove the hard drive connector.**

5. Unplug the battery from the logic board (see Figure 5-21).
6. Remove the battery from the iPod (see Figure 5-22).

Figure 5-22: **Remove the battery.**

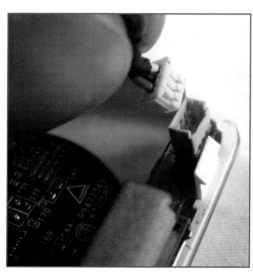

Figure 5-21: **Unplug the battery.**

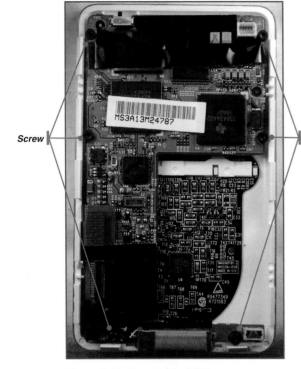

Figure 5-23: Remove the T6 Torx screws.

7. With your T6 Torx screwdriver, remove all six screws from the logic board (see Figure 5-23).

8. Remove the logic board from the front of the iPod (see Figure 5-24). A connector holds the logic board in place. There's no special technique here; just unplug the connector.

Figure 5-24: Remove the logic board.

9. Notice the back of the screen. Unplug the screen from the front of the iPod, and remove the screen (see Figure 5-25).

10. Plug in the new screen.

11. Plug the logic board back into the front of the iPod.

12. Replace all six T6 Torx screws.

13. Plug the battery back into the logic board.

14. Plug the hard drive connector back into the logic board.

Figure 5-25: Unplug the screen.

15. Slide the hard drive back into the connector.

16. Plug the audio jack back in.

17. Snap the iPod back together.

Replace the Screen in a Fourth-Generation iPod or an iPod Photo

To replace the screen in a fourth-generation monochrome iPod or an iPod photo:

1. Open the iPod according to the instructions in Chapter 3.

2. Unplug the audio jack from the logic board (see Figure 5-26).

3. Slide the hard drive from the hard drive connector, and remove the hard drive from the iPod.

4. Unplug the battery from the logic board, and remove the battery (see Figure 5-27).

Figure 5-26: *Unplug the audio jack.*

Figure 5-28: *Remove the tape.*

Figure 5-27: *Remove the battery.*

5. Remove the black tape covering the hard drive connector (see Figure 5-28). Keep this piece of tape, because you'll need it later.

6. See those exposed T6 Torx screws? There are six of them in a fourth-generation monochrome iPod, and there are five of them in an iPod photo. With your T6 Torx screwdriver, remove them all (see Figure 5-29).

7. Unclip the ribbon cable connecting the Click Wheel to the logic board (see Figure 5-30). This is the ribbon cable on the bottom.

Screw 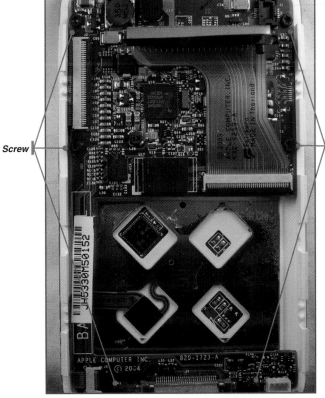 **Screw**

*Figure 5-29: **Remove the T6 Torx screws.***

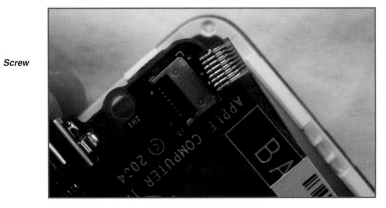

*Figure 5-30: **Unclip the Click Wheel's ribbon cable.***

8. Unclip the ribbon cable connecting the screen to the logic board (see Figure 5-31). This is the ribbon cable on the top.

Connector

*Figure 5-31: **Unclip the screen's ribbon cable.***

Figure 5-32: *Remove the logic board.*

9. Remove the logic board from the iPod (see Figure 5-32).

10. Pull the screen from the iPod (see Figure 5-33).

Figure 5-33: *Remove the screen.*

11. Put the new screen in place.

12. Put the logic board back in.

13. Connect the new screen to the logic board.

14. Reconnect the Click Wheel to the logic board.

15. Replace all the T6 Torx screws.

16. Plug the battery back into the logic board.

17. Replace the black tape over the hard drive connector.

18. Plug the audio jack back in.

19. Put the iPod back together.

Replace the Screen in an iPod Video

To replace the screen in a fifth-generation iPod:

1. Open the iPod according to the instructions in Chapter 3.

2. At the bottom of the unit, find and disconnect the ribbon cable from the battery (see Figure 5-34). Be sure to pull the cable near its connection point; don't use the fingers in the figure as a guide. There is a brown clip that you can pull up to make the cable easier to remove. Be gentle with this clip, though, as it can pop off.

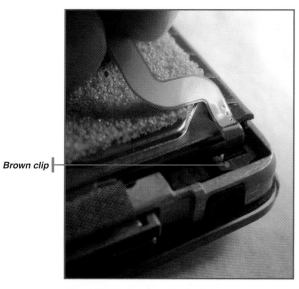

Brown clip

Figure 5-34: *Remove the battery cable.*

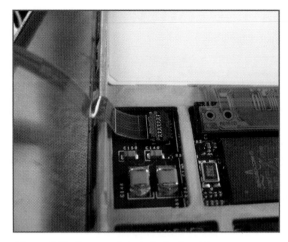

*Figure 5-35: **Remove the audio jack cable.***

3. Find and disconnect the ribbon cable from the audio jack (see Figure 5-35). This connector also has a brown clip that works like the one in step 2.

4. Carefully lift the hard drive and rotate the hard drive out of the iPod casing, disconnect it using the black clip, and remove it (see Figure 5-36).

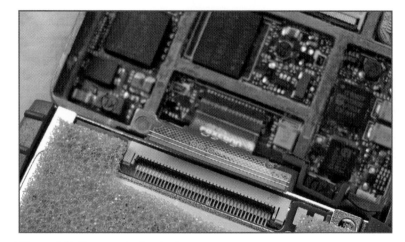

*Figure 5-36: **Remove the hard drive.***

5. Once the hard drive is removed, unclip the screen from the logic board (see Figure 5-37). Use the brown clip as needed.

6. Notice the six Phillips-head screws—three on each side—that hold the front of the iPod to the frame. Remove all six screws (see Figure 5-38).

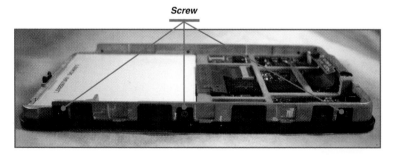

*Figure 5-38: **Remove the screws.***

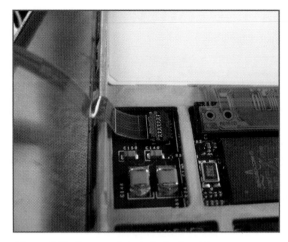

*Figure 5-37: **Unclip the screen.***

7. Separate the front of the iPod from the screen and the logic board (see Figure 5-39).

*Figure 5-39: **Remove the front of the iPod.***

8. Pull the screen out of the logic board (see Figure 5-40).

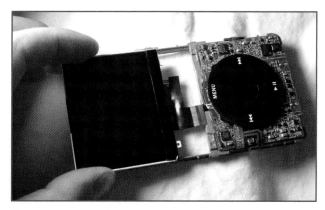

*Figure 5-40: **Remove the screen.***

9. Put the new screen where the old one was.

10. Put the front of the iPod back onto the frame.

11. Replace the six Phillips-head screws.

12. Clip the screen's ribbon connector down.

13. Plug the hard drive back into the hard drive connector.

14. Reattach the audio jack ribbon cable into the connector on the logic board.

15. Rotate the hard drive, and place it in the iPod.

16. Plug the battery's ribbon cable back into the logic board.

17. Put the iPod back together.

Replace Your iPod Mini's Screen

If your iPod mini's screen is giving you trouble, you don't have to grin and bear it. Exercise your First Amendment rights and replace it. Table 5-2 shows the required tools and the difficulty level.

iPOD MINI MODEL	TOOLS NEEDED	DIFFICULTY LEVEL
First-generation iPod mini	iPod-opening tools or flat-headed screwdriver and small Phillips-head screwdriver	Moderate
Second-generation iPod mini	iPod-opening tools or flat-headed screwdriver and small Phillips-head screwdriver	Moderate

Table 5-2: **Tools Needed and Difficulty Level of Replacing the Screen in an iPod Mini**

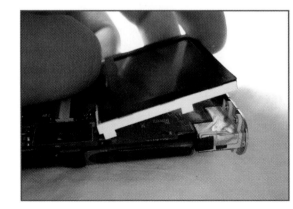

Figure 5-41: **Unclip the screen.**

To replace the screen in a first- or second-generation iPod mini, follow these steps:

1. Open the iPod according to the instructions in Chapter 3.

2. Four clips—two per side—attach the screen to the iPod mini. Unclip them to release the screen (see Figure 5-41).

3. The screen is connected to the logic board by ribbon cable, which is slid into a small, brown clip. Release the brown clip, and the ribbon cable slides out easily (see Figure 5-42).

4. Connect the new screen, and clip it back into place on the logic board.

5. Slide the logic board back into the shell.

*Figure 5-42: **Disconnect the screen's ribbon cable.***

Cable

Connector

6. Plug the Click Wheel back into the logic board.

7. Put the screws back in the top.

8. Replace the metal clip at the bottom of the iPod mini.

9. Replace the plastic pieces on the top and bottom of the iPod mini.

Replace Your iPod Nano's Screen

We turn now to the iPod nano. You'll recall from Chapter 4 that the nano isn't the easiest component to fix, so, as you might expect, replacing the screen is on the tricky side (see Table 5-3). Fortunately, you don't have to solder anything this time around. If you read all the instructions thoroughly beforehand and take the repair work nice and slow, you shouldn't run into problems.

iPOD NANO MODEL	TOOLS NEEDED	DIFFICULTY LEVEL
First-generation iPod nano	iPod-opening tools or flat-headed screwdriver and small Phillips-head screwdriver	Hard
Second-generation iPod nano	iPod-opening tools or flat-headed screwdriver and small Phillips-head screwdriver	Very hard

*Table 5-3: **Tools Needed and Difficulty Level of Replacing the Screen in an iPod Nano***

Replace the Screen in a First-Generation iPod Nano

To replace the screen in a first-generation iPod nano:

1. Open the iPod according to the instructions in Chapter 3.

2. Three screws hold down the logic board. With your Phillips-head screwdriver, remove these screws (see Figure 5-43).

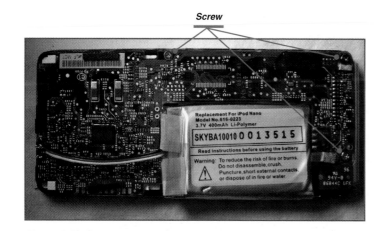

*Figure 5-43: **Remove the screws.***

Screw

*Figure 5-44: **Release the battery.***

3. Release the battery from the logic board (see Figure 5-44). Use your iPod-opening tool, because the battery is glued down. Do *not* completely remove the battery from the logic board, because it is soldered in place.

4. Carefully pull the screen from the front panel (see Figure 5-45). The screen is glued down with adhesive.

5. Notice the ribbon cable that connects the front of the iPod nano to the logic board. Release the clip, and unplug this ribbon cable to free the logic board (see Figure 5-46). Then pull the logic board from the iPod nano.

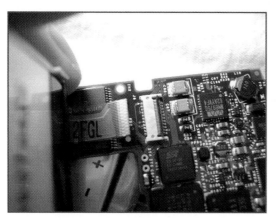

*Figure 5-45: **Pull off the screen.***

Clip

*Figure 5-46: **Remove the ribbon cable, and pull out the logic board.***

6. Release the side clips that hold the screen to the logic board (see Figure 5-47). There are two on each side. You should be able to use your fingers.

*Figure 5-47: **Unclip the screen.***

7. Locate the ribbon cable that connects the screen to the logic board, and unclip this ribbon cable (see Figure 5-48).

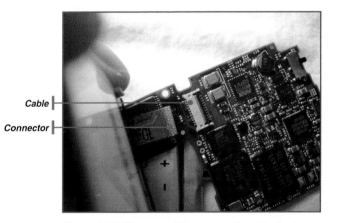

*Figure 5-48: **Disconnect the screen from the logic board.***

8. Attach the new screen to the logic board, and plug the ribbon cable into its connector.

9. Plug the Click Wheel's ribbon cable back into the logic board.

10. Place the logic board back into the iPod nano.

11. Replace the three screws.

12. Put the iPod nano back together.

Replace the Screen in a Second-Generation iPod Nano

To replace the screen in a second-generation iPod nano:

1. Open the iPod according to the instructions in Chapter 3.

2. With your iPod-opening tool or flat-headed screwdriver, carefully remove the screen from the metal bracket (see Figure 5-49).

3. Unclip the screen from the logic board, and remove the screen from the iPod nano (see Figure 5-50).

4. Plug the orange ribbon cable into the new screen.

5. Attach the new screen to the metal bracket.

6. Carefully slide the logic board back into the casing.

7. Reattach the audio jack to the logic board.

8. Replace the screw under the audio jack.

9. Place the metal bracket back into the bottom of the iPod nano.

10. Slide the audio jack back into place.

11. Replace the bottom and then the top screws.

12. Put the top and bottom plastic pieces back into place.

Figure 5-49: *Remove the screen from the metal bracket.*

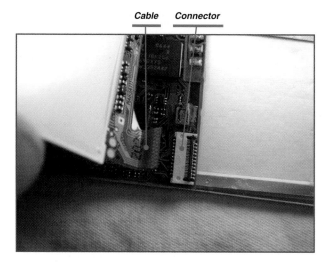

Cable   Connector

Figure 5-50: *Unclip the screen from the logic board.*

How to...

- **Get a New Hard Drive**

- **Replace the Hard Drive in a First- or Second-Generation iPod**

- **Replace the Hard Drive in a Third-Generation iPod**

- **Replace the Hard Drive in a Fourth-Generation iPod or an iPod Photo**

- **Replace the Hard Drive in an iPod Video**

- **Put the iPod Mini into Disk Mode**

Chapter 6
Storing Tunes and Such: Sorting Out Your Hard Drive

The hard drive is perhaps the most crucial component of your iPod, because that's where it stores your music files. If your hard drive goes rogue on you, you can't listen to your tunes, in which case your iPod becomes a very expensive (if stylish) keychain ornament. Replacing a bad hard drive gets you back into the groove. We show you how in this chapter.

This chapter also marks the first opportunity for you to put your iPod through a little elective surgery. Even if your hard drive is functioning perfectly, you might consider replacing it anyway with a newer, higher-capacity drive. It's often cheaper than buying a brand-new iPod. In fact, if you don't mind getting your hands dirty, you can upgrade your iPod's storage capacity beyond the highest factory rating. How's that for a personalized lifestyle gadget?

Check the Signs of a Bad Hard Drive

Hard drives go bad from wear and tear. The disks, or *platters*, inside a hard drive physically spin at an insane rate of speed, which is 3,600 times per minute on the *slow* side. Before you've used your iPod for five hours, the platters might have spun a million times. After about a year of regular use, they've spun a billion times. And that's just with the slowpokes. Faster iPod hard drives spin 4,200 times per minute, while computer hard drives can spin as fast as 7,200, 10,000, or 15,000 times per minute.

How do you know if your iPod's hard drive is shot? If your iPod shows the sad iPod face, there's a good chance that a bad hard drive is the cause. You should scan the hard drive to make sure.

Occasionally, when you're loading music to your iPod, it slows down or stops loading altogether. This might also indicate that your hard drive is bad, but scan the hard drive before you arrive at that conclusion.

A less subjective way to tell if your hard drive is shot is to put your iPod up to your ear and listen to it. A bad hard drive often makes a lot of noise, from a rapid clicking to a kind of grinding. Sometimes this noise is really loud. If you've ever heard it, you know exactly what it sounds like. Marc will never forget that sound for as long as he lives, because it was the sound of his data going bye-bye. You know, the data that he didn't adequately back up.

Scan Your Hard Drive

Scanning your hard drive is, by far, the best way to tell if your iPod is experiencing hard drive issues. The scan should always be step one when you suspect that the hard drive is bad. Don't go out and buy a replacement drive until you've completed the scan. It does you no good to pop in a new hard drive when the old one wasn't the problem; imagine your surprise when the iPod has the same stupid issue after you go to the trouble of replacing the hard drive.

To scan your hard drive:

1. Put the iPod into diagnostic mode. See Chapter 2 for complete instructions.
2. Use the **Forward** and **Reverse** buttons to navigate the menu choices until you get to HDD Scan.
3. Press the **Select** button to start the scan.

Make yourself comfortable, because this could take a while. A hard drive scan sets you back 15 minutes to an hour for most models. Occasionally, it takes longer.

When the scan finishes, your iPod returns *HDD Scan Pass* or *HDD Scan Fail*. Failure indicates a bad hard drive, so go ahead and replace her. If the hard drive passes, you need to look elsewhere for the source of your problems. Your iPod's logic board is the primary suspect now; see Chapter 9 for how to proceed.

Check for Drive Compatibility

Of all the many hard drives on the market today, only a few models are iPod-compatible, while those that work in certain kind of iPods don't work in others.

You can divide iPod-compatible hard drives into two categories: OEM and non-OEM drives. *OEM* stands for Original Equipment Manufacturer. An OEM hard drive, then, is one of the actual hard drives that Apple buys wholesale and installs in the iPod at the factory. If you're going to replace your iPod's hard drive, you might as well use the same components that Apple does, maximizing compatibility and minimizing your headache. (As you'll see momentarily, though, there are reasons why you might consider going the non-OEM route.)

Table 6-1 lists the OEM hard drives. As you review your options, keep in mind that you don't have to put in the exact same hard drive that you take out. Any OEM hard drive is as good as any other, just as long as it's compatible with your generation of iPod.

Non-OEM hard drives don't come with any factory-made iPod, but they're compatible with the iPod nevertheless. What makes non-OEM hard drives

CAPACITY AND TYPE	BRAND	MODEL NUMBER	COMPATIBILITY
4-gigabyte (GB) Microdrive	Hitachi	HMS360404D5CF00	First- and second-generation iPod mini
	Seagate	ST640211CF	
6-GB Microdrive	Hitachi	HMS360606D5CF00	Released for the second-generation iPod mini, but also works in the first-generation iPod mini
	Seagate	ST660211CF	
5-GB hard drive	Toshiba	MK5002MAL	First- and second-generation iPods
10-GB hard drive	Toshiba	MK1003GAL	First-, second-, and third-generation iPods
15-GB hard drive	Toshiba	MK1504GAL	Released for the third-generation iPods, but also works in the fourth-generation monochrome iPod
20-GB hard drive	Toshiba	MK2003GAH	Second-generation iPod
	Toshiba	MK2004GAL	Third- and fourth-generation monochrome iPods, iPod photo (fourth-generation color iPod)
	Toshiba	MK2006GAL	Fourth-generation monochrome iPod, iPod photo (fourth-generation color iPod)
30-GB hard drive	Toshiba	MK3006GAL	Released for the iPod photo (fourth-generation color iPod), but also works in the fourth-generation monochrome iPod
	Toshiba	MK3008GAL	iPod video (fifth-generation iPod)
40-GB hard drive	Toshiba	MK4004GAH	Third- and fourth-generation monochrome iPods, iPod photo (fourth-generation color iPod)
	Toshiba	MK4006GAH	Fourth-generation monochrome iPod, iPod photo (fourth-generation color iPod)
60-GB hard drive	Toshiba	MK6006GAH	Released for the iPod photo, but also works with the fourth-generation monochrome iPod
	Toshiba	MK6008GAH	iPod video (fifth-generation iPod)
80-GB hard drive	Toshiba	MK8010GAH	iPod video (fifth-generation iPod)

Table 6-1: *OEM Hard Drives for the iPod and iPod Mini*

GET A NEW HARD DRIVE

Hard drives aren't always easy to buy off the shelf at the local mall, but doing an Internet search for the specific model number of the drive that you want turns up all kinds of buying opportunities.

A replacement hard drive for your iPod costs around $100 to $200 U.S., depending on the model and the vendor. You might run across some juicy deals on eBay, so keep your eyes open.

Our technical editor points out that if you go the eBay route, you don't necessarily have to buy new. You could conceivably acquire a second-hand hard drive at a fraction of the cost of a brand-new component. As long as the hard drive is in good working order (and as long as it's one of the compatible models for your iPod), you can use it for your replacement drive. Of course, you get into stickier issues of quality assurance and customer satisfaction whenever you deal in the second-hand market, especially where high-tech components are concerned. *Buyer beware* most definitely applies.

As you consider your options, your high school economics class will serve you well. There's a point at which the cost of your replacement drive plus the time you spend installing it are together more expensive than the cost of a brand-new iPod. Keep in mind also that the data from your old drive must be transferred to the new one, so even by replacing the drive, you're getting what amounts to a brand-new iPod. Perhaps the only way you truly come out on top is if you put in a higher-capacity drive than you take out. But if the time spent isn't worth it, then just buy a new iPod. That's what Steve Jobs would want of you anyway.

desirable is their greater storage capacity. For instance, you can get 8 GB of storage in an iPod mini by using a non-OEM hard drive, while you can bump up your fifth-generation iPod to 100 GB. (The highest from-the-factory ratings are 6 GB and 80 GB, respectively.) Some non-OEM hard drives are technically iPod-compatible, but they require hacks before they're usable.

Table 6-2 lists two recommended non-OEM hard drives, neither of which requires special hacks to install.

CAPACITY AND TYPE	BRAND	MODEL NUMBER	COMPATIBILITY
8-GB Microdrive	Seagate	ST68022C-RK	First- and second-generation iPod mini
100-GB hard drive	Toshiba	MK1011GAH	iPod video (fifth-generation iPod)

Table 6-2: **Recommended Non-OEM Hard Drives for the iPod and iPod Mini**

Replace Your iPod's Hard Drive

Table 6-3 shows the required tools and the difficulty level of replacing the hard drive in an iPod. We discuss the iPod mini later in this chapter.

iPOD MODEL	TOOLS NEEDED	DIFFICULTY LEVEL
First-generation iPod	iPod-opening tools or flat-headed screwdriver	Moderate
Second-generation iPod	iPod-opening tools or flat-headed screwdriver	Moderate
Third-generation iPod	iPod-opening tools or flat-headed screwdriver	Moderate
Fourth-generation iPod (monochrome)	iPod-opening tools or flat-headed screwdriver	Moderate
iPod photo (fourth-generation color iPod)	iPod-opening tools or flat-headed screwdriver	Moderate
iPod video (fifth-generation iPod)	iPod-opening tools or flat-headed screwdriver	Moderate

Table 6-3: **Tools Needed and Difficulty Level for Replacing the Hard Drive in an iPod**

Figure 6-1: *Disconnect the hard drive.*

Replace the Hard Drive in a First- or Second-Generation iPod

To replace the hard drive in a first- or second-generation iPod:

1. Open your iPod according to the instructions in Chapter 3.

2. Unplug and remove the battery from the iPod.

3. Slide the hard drive from the orange hard drive connector (see Figure 6-1). Just use your fingers.

4. Remove the hard drive from the iPod, and remove the pieces of rubber that protect the hard drive (see Figure 6-2).

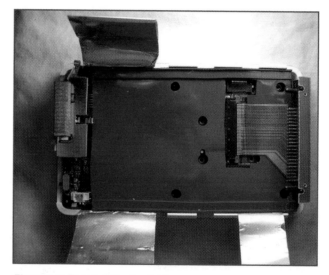

Figure 6-2: *Remove the hard drive.*

5. Put the pieces of rubber on the new hard drive.

6. Slide the new hard drive into the connector (see Figure 6-3).

7. Put the iPod back together.

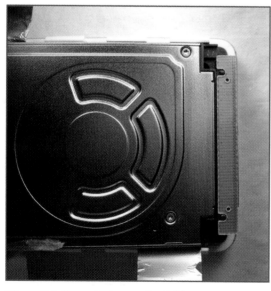

Figure 6-3: *Connect the new hard drive.*

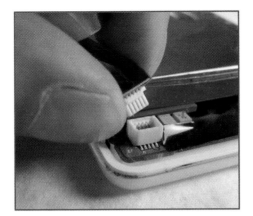

*Figure 6-4: **Disconnect the audio jack.***

Replace the Hard Drive in a Third-Generation iPod

To replace the hard drive in a third-generation iPod:

1. Open your iPod according to the instructions in Chapter 3.
2. Disconnect the audio jack from the logic board (see Figure 6-4).
3. Locate the hard drive.
4. Slide the hard drive from the hard drive connector.
5. Remove the hard drive from the iPod, and remove the pieces of rubber that protect the hard drive.
6. Put the pieces of rubber on the new hard drive.
7. Plug the new hard drive into the hard drive connector.
8. Plug in the audio jack.
9. Put the iPod back together.

NOTE

The rear casing of the 30-GB iPod video is slightly different from that of the 60-GB and 80-GB versions, because the 30-GB hard drive is physically smaller than the other drives. If you're upgrading your iPod video's 30-GB hard drive to something with more storage space (including the 100-GB non-OEM option), you need to replace the rear casing, too, to accommodate the larger drive. If you already have a 60-GB or 80-GB iPod video, you already have the right casing, unless, of course, you're downgrading your iPod to 30-GB for some strange reason known only to you. Occasionally, Brandon offers iPod casings for sale on www.Synctogo.com, but you might also try a general Internet search. Many iPod repair services keep them in stock.

Replace the Hard Drive in a Fourth-Generation iPod or an iPod Photo

To replace the hard drive in a fourth-generation monochrome iPod or an iPod photo:

1. Open your iPod according to the instructions in Chapter 3.
2. Disconnect the audio jack from the logic board (see Figure 6-5).

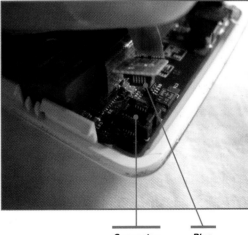

*Figure 6-5: **Disconnect the audio jack.***

Connector   **Plug**

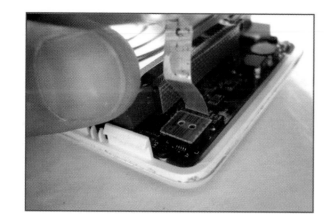

Figure 6-6: *Plug in the audio jack.*

3. Locate the hard drive.

4. Slide the hard drive from the orange hard drive connector.

5. Remove the hard drive from the iPod, and remove the pieces of blue rubber that protect the hard drive.

6. Put the pieces of rubber on the new hard drive.

7. Slide the new hard drive into the hard drive connector.

8. Plug the audio jack back into the logic board (see Figure 6-6).

9. Put the iPod back together.

Replace the Hard Drive in an iPod Video

To replace the hard drive in a fifth-generation iPod or iPod Video:

1. Open your iPod according to the instructions in Chapter 3.

2. Unplug the battery from its connector (see Figure 6-7). To help you loosen the connection, you can slide the brown clip.

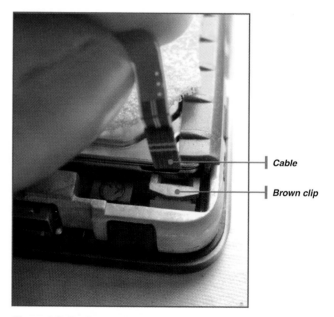

Cable

Brown clip

Figure 6-7: *Unplug the battery.*

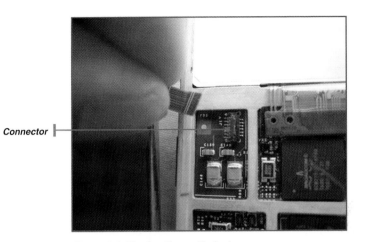

Connector ⊢

Figure 6-8: **Unplug the audio jack.**

3. Rotate the hard drive to unplug the audio jack's ribbon cable from the logic board (see Figure 6-8).

4. Locate the hard drive.

5. Find the small connector that holds the hard drive to the logic board (see Figure 6-9).

6. Pull up the black clip to release the hard drive from its connector.

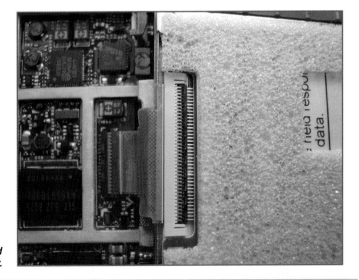

Figure 6-9: **Find the hard drive connector.**

Figure 6-10: *Release the hard drive from its connector.*

7. Remove the hard drive from the iPod, and remove the pieces of blue or grey rubber that protect the hard drive (see Figure 6-10).

8. Put the pieces of rubber on the new hard drive.

9. Plug in the new hard drive.

10. Plug in the ribbon cable for the audio jack.

11. Plug in the ribbon cable for the battery (see Figure 6-11).

12. Put the iPod back together.

Figure 6-11: *Plug in the battery.*

Replace Your iPod Mini's Hard Drive

Table 6-4 shows the required tools and the difficulty level of replacing the hard drive in an iPod mini.

iPOD MINI MODEL	TOOLS NEEDED	DIFFICULTY LEVEL
First-generation iPod mini	iPod-opening tools or flat-headed screwdriver	Moderate
Second-generation iPod mini	iPod-opening tools or flat-headed screwdriver	Moderate

Table 6-4: *Tools Needed and Difficulty Level for Replacing the Hard Drive in an iPod Mini*

To replace the hard drive in a first- or second-generation iPod mini:

1. Open your iPod mini according to the instructions in Chapter 3.

2. Locate the mini's Microdrive on the backside of the logic board. It's the component with *Microdrive* printed on it.

3. Unplug the Microdrive from the logic board (see Figure 6-12).

4. Plug the new Microdrive into the logic board.

5. Slide the logic board back into the mini's shell (see Figure 6-13).

TIP

After you replace your iPod mini's Microdrive, you need to put the mini into Disk Mode and then restore the mini in iTunes. See the "Putting the iPod Mini into Disk Mode" QuickSteps for more information.

Figure 6-12: **Unplug the Microdrive.**

Figure 6-13: **Slide in the logic board.**

6. Reconnect the Click Wheel (see Figure 6-14).

Figure 6-14: **Reconnect the Click Wheel.**

7. Replace the two screws in the top of the mini (see Figure 6-15).

8. Place the metal clip back onto the bottom of the mini (see Figure 6-16).

Figure 6-15: **Replace the screws.**

Figure 6-16: **Replace the metal clip.**

Figure 6-17: **Replace the plastic pieces.**

9. Replace the plastic pieces on the top and bottom of the mini (see Figure 6-17).

QUICKSTEPS

PUT THE iPOD MINI INTO DISK MODE

After you replace the Microdrive in an iPod mini, you need to put the mini into Disk Mode before you can restore it in iTunes. If you don't do this, your mini won't function correctly.

To put your iPod mini into Disk Mode:

1. Hold down the **Menu** and **Select** buttons for about five to eight seconds to reset your iPod mini.

2. The mini shuts down and starts up again almost immediately. When the Apple logo appears on the screen, hold down the **Back** and **Select** buttons until you see the backwards Apple logo and hear an audible chirp.

3. The mini prompts you to press the Play button to continue. Press **Play**. You now have access to the diagnostic menu.

4. Browse the menu for the Diskmode option. Highlight it, and press the **Select** button to select it.

You can now restore your iPod mini in iTunes.

Restore Your iPod in iTunes

When you turn on your iPod for the first time after installing a new hard drive, you will probably see the folder icon, which indicates software issues. What's happening is that your iPod is looking for its operating system on the new hard drive. Unless the operating system came preinstalled, it won't be there for the iPod to find.

Before you can use your iPod, you must copy the operating system software to the new hard drive, which means restoring the iPod in iTunes, so connect your iPod to your computer and follow the on-screen prompts.

You should also copy your backed-up music files to your new hard drive. Once your iPod is restored, iTunes asks you to sync your iPod, just like you did when you bought it brand-new. During this process, your tunes are loaded to their new home. As soon as syncing completes, you're good to go.

Chapter 7

Cranking Up the Volume: Replacing Your Audio Jack

When legendary house band M|A|R|R|S enjoins you to pump up the volume, pump up the volume, pump up the volume, dance, dance, we defy you to do anything but. That is, of course, if you can hear them. If you can't, your iPod's audio jack might need some attention. In this chapter, we show you how to replace the audio jack so that you can get back to the business of cranking it up to 11.

Check the Signs of a Bad Audio Jack

Good old-fashioned wear and tear is the usual reason for audio jack failure. There's typically some sort of connection problem. Electrical impulses travel from your iPod to your earbuds by way of the audio jack, which acts more or

less like a doorway. The impulses go out through the audio jack into the wire that feeds your earbuds, which are nothing more than very small speakers. Their function is to convert the impulses to sound. If something breaks down anywhere along this connection, the impulses never reach your earbuds or they arrive in a damaged or incomplete state.

Despite whatever your mom might have told you, playing your music too loud doesn't really have anything to do with it. While loud music can most definitely fry your earbuds or speakers—as well as permanently damage your hearing—it doesn't have an effect on the audio jack itself.

What does bad audio sound like? Distorted sound, dropouts, and static top the list. Also, if you have stereo problems—that is, if audio is coming out of one earbud and not the other—the audio jack might be to blame. No sound at all is equally suspect.

However, don't conclude that you need to replace your audio jack until you've double-checked your earbuds. Bad audio by itself indicates a bad connection, but the audio jack isn't the only place that the connection can go bad. A pinched, severed, or blown-out wire inside the earbud cable can cause exactly the same sorts of symptoms. So always try to solve your audio problems first by plugging in a different set of earbuds or headphones, or test your earbuds on another device with a headphone jack, such as your computer.

Replace Your iPod's Audio Jack

Table 7-1 shows the required tools and the difficulty level of replacing the audio jack in an iPod. We discuss the iPod mini and the iPod nano in subsequent sections of this chapter.

The bad news first: In first- and second-generation iPods, the audio jack is soldered to the logic board. Replacing the audio jack by itself is a bit too hard for someone without a lot of iPod repair experience, so we don't provide instructions here. However, this doesn't mean that you're stuck without a

QUICKFACTS

GETTING A NEW AUDIO JACK

You can buy a replacement audio jack online from most any iPod repair service. Do an Internet search or visit Brandon at www.Synctogo.com. You might also have some luck on eBay.

Prices range from about 20 bucks to 60 bucks U.S., depending on which iPod model you're repairing.

iPOD MODEL	TOOLS NEEDED	DIFFICULTY LEVEL
First-generation iPod	Not advised	Do not attempt; replace the logic board instead
Second-generation iPod	Not advised	Do not attempt; replace the logic board instead
Third-generation iPod	iPod-opening tools or flat-headed screwdriver and small Phillips-head screwdriver	Easy
Fourth-generation iPod (monochrome)	iPod-opening tools or flat-headed screwdriver and small Phillips-head screwdriver	Easy
iPod photo (fourth-generation color iPod)	iPod-opening tools or flat-headed screwdriver and small Phillips-head screwdriver	Easy
iPod video (fifth-generation iPod)	iPod-opening tools or flat-headed screwdriver and small Phillips-head screwdriver	Moderate

Table 7-1: **Tools Needed and Difficulty Level for Replacing the Audio Jack in an iPod**

do-it-yourself solution. To clear up your audio issues, you can simply replace the entire logic board, including the audio jack. It might seem strange or counterintuitive, but it's actually much easier (and safer) to swap logic boards than it is to fiddle around with the audio jack and a soldering iron.

To replace your iPod's logic board, see Chapter 9 of this book.

Replace the Audio Jack in a Third- or Fourth-Generation iPod or an iPod Photo

To replace the audio jack in a third- or fourth-generation monochrome iPod or an iPod photo:

1. Open the iPod according to the instructions in Chapter 3.

2. Disconnect the audio jack from the logic board (see Figure 7-1).

Figure 7-1: **Disconnect the audio jack.**

3. Remove the back from the iPod (see Figure 7-2).

Figure 7-2: **Remove the back.**

4. Locate the audio jack on the back piece (see Figure 7-3).

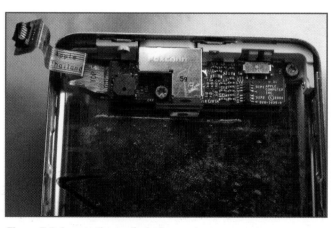

Figure 7-3: **Locate the audio jack.**

5. There are three screws attaching the audio jack to the frame of the iPod. Take out all three screws with your Phillips-head screwdriver (see Figure 7-4).

Screw

Figure 7-4: **Remove the screws.**

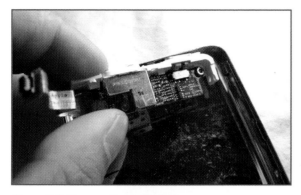

Figure 7-5: *Remove the audio jack.*

Brown clip

Figure 7-6: *Unplug the battery.*

Figure 7-8: *Unplug the audio jack.*

6. Remove the audio jack (see Figure 7-5). You might have to pull gently, as a small bit of adhesive holds the audio jack in place.

7. Put in the new audio jack.

8. Replace all three screws.

9. Plug the audio jack back into the logic board.

10. Put the iPod back together.

Replace the Audio Jack in an iPod Video

To replace the audio jack in a fifth-generation iPod:

1. Open your iPod according to the instructions in Chapter 3.

2. A ribbon cable connects the battery to the logic board. Unplug it (see Figure 7-6). Pull up gently on the brown clip, and the cable should easily come loose.

3. Rotate the hard drive out of the iPod (see Figure 7-7).

Figure 7-7: *Rotate the hard drive.*

4. Locate the audio jack's ribbon cable. Pull up gently on the brown clip to release this cable, and then unplug it (see Figure 7-8).

5. Locate the battery on the back of the iPod, and remove it (see Figure 7-9). A little bit of adhesive holds it in place.

Figure 7-9: **Remove the battery.**

6. There are four screws holding the audio jack in place. Remove all four screws with your Phillips-head screwdriver.

7. Find the little piece of black tape that holds down part of the ribbon cable. Remove this tape (see Figure 7-10).

Figure 7-10: **Remove the screws and the tape.**

Figure 7-11: **Put in the new audio jack.**

8. Place the new audio jack in the iPod (see Figure 7-11).

9. Replace all four screws.

10. Reapply the black tape just as you found it.

QUICK**FACTS**

BALANCING AUDIO QUALITY AND STORAGE SPACE

Out of convenience or habit, you might call your iPod an MP3 player, but it can play other kinds of music files, too.

Perhaps the most common alternate format is AAC, or Advanced Audio Coding. In fact, Apple would like you to think of the iPod as an AAC player, not as an MP3 player, because AACs are what Apple sells on iTunes. Technically speaking, an AAC file is very similar to an MP3, so much so that it's not entirely incorrect to think of AAC as MP3 version 2.0. Proponents of AAC tout its many improvements over the MP3 format, but MP3 has at least one major advantage: popularity. MP3 is far and away more successful than AAC in terms of sheer numbers of users, and while MP3 has slipped into the nontechnical vernacular, AAC has, as yet, not, no matter how bad Steve Jobs might want it to happen.

At the beginning of this chapter, we mentioned that MP3s—and by extension AACs—tend to lack in the fidelity department, but we didn't really tell you why. Part of the reason is the level of compression in the typical MP3. Raw digital audio takes up a lot of storage space. The audio data need to be crushed down into smaller, more manageable files if you want to be able to carry around thousands of songs. That's where the MP3 format comes in. It makes the audio much more compact by putting it through a process of *compression*. The form of compression in an MP3—*lossy* compression, as it's called—gets rid of some of the excess data, which causes an audible drop in quality. Normally, most ears can't tell much of a difference, but the discerning ear can, and the loss in quality becomes obvious to everyone when the rate of compression goes too high.

There is such a thing as *lossless* compression, which stores audio information more efficiently without getting

Continued . . .

11. Place the battery back in the iPod.

12. Reconnect the audio jack's ribbon cable. Make sure the brown clip is clipped down on the cable.

13. Rotate the hard drive back into the iPod.

14. Reconnect the battery's ribbon cable. Again, make sure the brown clip is pressed down.

15. Put the iPod back together.

Replace Your iPod Mini's Audio Jack

Table 7-2 shows the required tools and the difficulty level of replacing the audio jack in an iPod mini.

iPOD MINI MODEL	TOOLS NEEDED	DIFFICULTY LEVEL
First-generation iPod mini	iPod-opening tools or flat-headed screwdriver and small Phillips-head screwdriver	Moderate
Second-generation iPod mini	iPod-opening tools or flat-headed screwdriver and small Phillips-head screwdriver	Moderate

Table 7-2: **Tools Needed and Difficulty Level for Replacing the Audio Jack in an iPod Mini**

To replace the audio jack in a first- or second-generation iPod mini:

1. Open your iPod mini according to the instructions in Chapter 3.

2. Locate the audio jack (see Figure 7-12). It's on the back side of the mini, just above the battery.

Figure 7-12: **Locate the audio jack.**

BALANCING AUDIO QUALITY AND STORAGE SPACE *(Continued)*

rid of any of the excess. Lossless compression gives you the best of both worlds. The data are compressed, so you can fit more songs onto your iPod, but no quality is lost, so the audio sounds exactly like the uncompressed original. Your iPod can play Apple Lossless files, which utilize just such a method of compression. The main drawback is that lossless compression doesn't crush down the audio as much as you might like. Apple Lossless files are generally larger than MP3s, although both are much smaller than uncompressed audio files.

Another snag with the Apple Lossless format in particular is its lack of portability to computers running Windows. If you want to play your tunes on your PC at work as well as on your iPod during the commute, the MP3 format makes more sense for purely practical reasons.

Your iPod is also capable of storing and playing pristine, uncompressed digital audio. On a Mac, uncompressed audio files reside in the AIFF format. On Windows, they're WAV files. We mention this for the sake of completeness, not as a recommendation. You're much better off with lossless compression. Lossless music sounds identical to AIFF and WAV while taking up considerably less storage. As a side note, you *can* listen to AIFF files on a computer running Windows, so if quality and multiplatform compatibility are equally important to you, uncompressed music is always an option.

Most people don't rate both factors equally. If your goal is to pack as much music on your iPod as you conceivably can, go with your old standby, the MP3, or try AAC, the iTunes alternative. But if you care less about quantity and more about quality (and if you can afford to snub the likes of Bill Gates), see about moving up to Apple Lossless format.

3. Carefully unplug the audio jack (see Figure 7-13). Watch out about applying too much force, because you can damage the logic board.

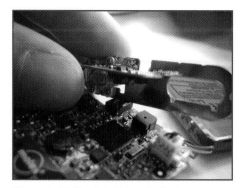

Figure 7-13: **Unplug the audio jack.**

4. Plug in the new audio jack (see Figure 7-14).

Figure 7-14: **Plug in the new audio jack.**

5. Slide the logic board and its contents back into the mini's shell.
6. Put the iPod back together.

Solve Your iPod Nano's Audio Problems

As you can see from Table 7-3, replacing the iPod nano's audio jack is not the sort of project that a non-pro should attempt. The reason? The audio jack is soldered to the logic board, and because the nano is that much smaller and more delicate than the iPod, the going is that much trickier. To be successful here, you really need to know what you're doing.

That said, you can solve your iPod nano's audio problems by installing a new logic board, audio jack and all. We show you how in Chapter 9.

iPOD NANO MODEL	TOOLS NEEDED	DIFFICULTY LEVEL
First-generation iPod nano	Not advised	Do not attempt; replace the logic board instead
Second-generation iPod nano	Not advised	Do not attempt; replace the logic board instead

Table 7-3: *Tools Needed and Difficulty Level for Replacing the Audio Jack in an iPod Nano*

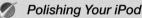
Chapter 8

Facing the Music: Replacing the Front Panel or Shell

You're always on the go, and you take your iPod with you. You shove it in your pocket. You toss it into your backpack. It rattles around in your gym bag on the subway. You take it out and pass it around to your friends. You've probably dropped it—more than once. Hopefully, you haven't put it through the washing machine.

Before long, that pearly, whiter-shade-of-pale surface that so enticed you in the gizmo store begins to look like the face of Frankenstein's monster. First it gets a little grungy. Then it picks up dings, dints, chips, and scratches, not to mention outright dents. It doesn't stop working. It plays just fine. It just looks like it's ready for some reconstructive surgery.

When this happens, Steve Jobs wants you to think about buying a new iPod. He believes that his customers are all about surface, and his next product generation is glittering in the display case. But you don't have to fall for his Apple-cult mind tricks. Why toss out a perfectly good iPod just because it's hideous-looking? Simply replace the original front panel or shell, and you get that fresh, shiny, new iPod look with none of the hassles of transferring your tunes. We show you how in this chapter.

Get a New Front Panel or Shell

You've decided to give your iPod a facelift. So do you need a new front panel, or do you need an entire shell? It all depends on your model of iPod. Table 8-1 spells it out for you.

You can buy front panels and shells from most iPod repair services, so check your existing favorite or do an Internet search. Brandon sells these items on

iPOD MODEL	PART NEEDED
First-generation iPod	Front panel
Second-generation iPod	Front panel
Third-generation iPod	Front panel
Fourth-generation iPod (monochrome)	Front panel
iPod photo (fourth-generation color iPod)	Front panel
iPod video (fifth-generation iPod)	Front panel
First-generation iPod mini	Shell
Second-generation iPod mini	Shell
First-generation iPod nano	Front panel
Second-generation iPod nano	Shell

*Table 8-1: **Whether to Replace the Front Panel or Shell of an iPod***

QUICKFACTS

POLISHING YOUR iPOD *(Continued)*

which he sells at www.Synctogo.com, and Apple Sauce Polish, which you can find at www.applesaucepolish.com. According to Brandon, these two systems work better than any of the others. You'll pay about 25 bucks for either one.

If you decide to try a polish, it's important to manage your expectations. The polish can work miracles with small or even moderate blemishes, but there are no guarantees, and you can forget about larger or deeper scratches. Decide for yourself what you want to achieve. If getting a pristine-looking iPod is a non-negotiable position for you, you're better off replacing the front panel or shell. If you just want to tidy up your iPod's appearance a little, the polish might be the better way to go.

www.Synctogo.com. You might also find a good deal on eBay, but that's hit or miss. Expect to pay $20 to $60 U.S., depending on the specific part that you need.

As always, make sure you're buying the correct front panel or shell. Every single generation of iPod has its own unique casing, and you can't mix and match.

Replace Your iPod's Front Panel

For the flagship iPod in all generations, the front panel is the part that you want to replace. Table 8-2 shows the required tools and the difficulty level. We talk about the iPod mini and the iPod nano later in this chapter.

Replace the Front Panel in a First-Generation iPod

To replace the front panel in a first-generation iPod:

1. Open the iPod according to the instructions in Chapter 3.
2. Pull the battery from the back of the hard drive (see Figure 8-1). There is adhesive holding it down.

iPOD MODEL	TOOLS NEEDED	DIFFICULTY LEVEL
First-generation iPod	iPod-opening tools or flat-headed screwdriver and T6 Torx screwdriver	Moderate
Second-generation iPod	iPod-opening tools or flat-headed screwdriver and T6 Torx screwdriver	Moderate
Third-generation iPod	iPod-opening tools or flat-headed screwdriver and T6 Torx screwdriver	Moderate
Fourth-generation iPod (monochrome)	iPod-opening tools or flat-headed screwdriver and T6 Torx screwdriver	Moderate
iPod photo (fourth-generation color iPod)	iPod-opening tools or flat-headed screwdriver and T6 Torx screwdriver	Moderate
iPod video (fifth-generation iPod)	iPod-opening tools or flat-headed screwdriver and T6 Torx screwdriver	Hard

*Table 8-2: **Tools Needed and Difficulty Level for Replacing the Front Panel in an iPod***

*Figure 8-1: **Pull the battery from the hard drive.***

3. Unplug the battery from the logic board (see Figure 8-2).

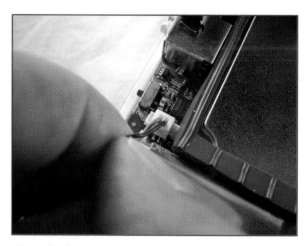

*Figure 8-2: **Unplug the battery.***

4. Carefully slide the hard drive from the orange hard drive connector.

5. Pull the hard drive from the iPod (see Figure 8-3).

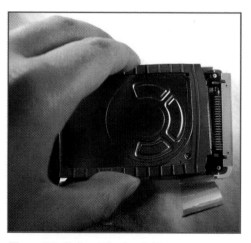

*Figure 8-3: **Pull out the hard drive.***

*Figure 8-4: **Remove the piece of rubber to expose all four T6 Torx screws.***

6. Find the four T6 Torx screws in the logic board. A large piece of rubber covers one of them. Take off this piece of rubber to expose the fourth screw (see Figure 8-4).

Figure 8-5: **Remove the T6 Torx screws.**

Screw

7. With your T6 Torx screwdriver, remove all four screws (see Figure 8-5).

8. Remove the logic board from the bottom of the iPod (see Figure 8-6). Now you should be left with the front panel only (see Figure 8-7).

Figure 8-6: **Remove the logic board.**

9. Place the logic board in your new front panel.

10. Replace all four T6 Torx screws in the logic board.

11. Slide the hard drive back into the hard drive connector.

12. Plug the battery back into the logic board.

13. Put the iPod back together.

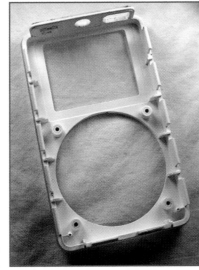

Figure 8-7: **Only the front panel remains.**

Replace the Front Panel
in a Second-Generation iPod

To replace the front panel in a second-generation iPod:

1. Open the iPod according to the instructions in Chapter 3.

2. Pull the battery from the back of the hard drive. There is adhesive holding it down.

3. Unplug the battery from the logic board.

4. Carefully slide the hard drive from the orange hard drive connector (see Figure 8-8.)

Figure 8-8: *Slide the hard drive from the connector.*

5. Notice the two small brown clips next to the hard drive connector. Pull down on them to loosen the connector, and remove it from the logic board (see Figure 8-9).

Figure 8-9: **Remove the hard drive connector.**

6. Pull the piece of blue rubber from the iPod (see Figure 8-10).

Figure 8-10: ***Pull out the piece of rubber.***

7. Loosen the scroll wheel's connector by pulling down on the brown tabs (see Figure 8-11).

8. Remove all eight T6 Torx screws from the logic board (see Figure 8-12).

Figure 8-11: ***Loosen the scroll wheel's connector.***

Screw

Figure 8-12: ***Remove the T6 Torx screws.***

9. Carefully lift the logic board just enough to release the scroll wheel's connector (see Figure 8-13).

Figure 8-13: **Release the scroll wheel's connector.**

10. Remove the logic board (see Figure 8-14). Now only the front panel of the iPod remains (see Figure 8-15).

Figure 8-14: **Remove the logic board.**

Figure 8-15: **Only the front panel remains.**

11. Place the logic board in the new front panel (see Figure 8-16).

12. Replace all eight T6 Torx screws.

*Figure 8-16: **Put the logic board into the new front panel.***

13. Plug in the scroll wheel's ribbon cable.

14. Reattach the hard drive connector, and place the piece of blue rubber where you found it.

15. Slide the hard drive into place.

16. Plug the battery into the logic board, and place the battery on top of the hard drive.

17. Put the iPod back together.

Replace the Front Panel in a Third-Generation iPod

To replace the front panel in a third-generation iPod:

1. Open the iPod according to the instructions in Chapter 3.

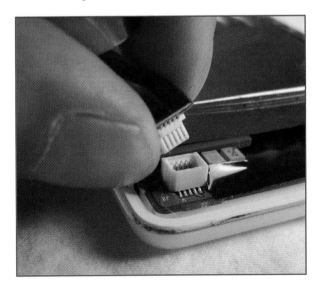

*Figure 8-17: **Unplug the audio jack.***

2. Unplug the audio jack from the logic board (see Figure 8-17).

3. Slide the hard drive from the hard drive connector, and remove the hard drive from the iPod (see Figure 8-18).

*Figure 8-18: **Remove the hard drive.***

Plug   Connector

Figure 8-19: *Remove the hard drive connector.*

Figure 8-20: *Unplug the battery.*

Figure 8-21: *Remove the battery.*

Screw   Screw

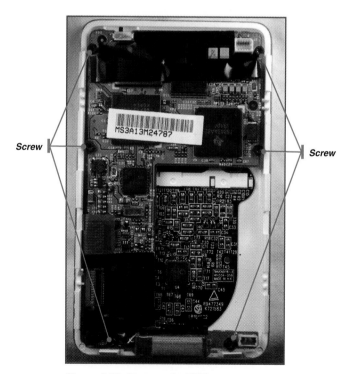

Figure 8-22: *Remove the T6 Torx screws.*

4. Unplug the hard drive connector from the logic board, and remove it from the iPod (see Figure 8-19).

5. Unplug the battery from the logic board (see Figure 8-20).

6. Remove the battery from the iPod (see Figure 8-21).

7. With your T6 Torx screwdriver, remove all six screws from the logic board (see Figure 8-22).

8. Remove the logic board from the front of the iPod (see Figure 8-23). A connector holds the logic board in place. Just unplug the connector.

Connector

Figure 8-23: *Remove the logic board.*

Figure 8-24: **Unplug the screen.**

9. Notice the back of the screen. Unplug the screen from the connector on the front of the iPod (see Figure 8-24). Now only the front panel of the iPod remains.

10. Plug the screen into the new front panel.

11. Plug the logic board into the new front panel.

12. Replace all six T6 Torx screws.

13. Plug the battery back into the logic board.

14. Plug the hard drive connector back into the logic board.

15. Slide the hard drive back into the connector.

16. Plug the audio jack back in.

17. Snap the iPod back together.

Replace the Front Panel in a Fourth-Generation iPod or an iPod Photo

To replace the front panel in a fourth-generation monochrome iPod or an iPod photo:

1. Open the iPod according to the instructions in Chapter 3.

2. Unplug the audio jack from the logic board (see Figure 8-25).

Figure 8-25: **Unplug the audio jack.**

Figure 8-26: **Remove the battery.**

Figure 8-27: **Remove the tape.**

3. Slide the hard drive from the hard drive connector, and remove the hard drive from the iPod.

4. Unplug the battery from the logic board, and remove the battery (see Figure 8-26).

5. Remove the black tape covering the hard drive connector (see Figure 8-27). Keep the tape, because you'll need it later.

6. Locate the exposed T6 Torx screws. There are six of them in a fourth-generation monochrome iPod, and there are five of them in an iPod photo. With your T6 Torx screwdriver, remove them all (see Figure 8-28).

Screw   Screw

Figure 8-28: **Remove the T6 Torx screws.**

Figure 8-29: **Unclip the Click Wheel's ribbon cable.**

7. Unclip the ribbon cable connecting the Click Wheel to the logic board (see Figure 8-29). This is the ribbon cable on the bottom.

8. Unclip the ribbon cable connecting the screen to the logic board (see Figure 8-30). This is the ribbon cable on the top.

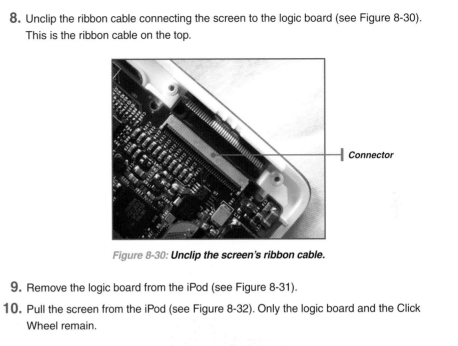

Figure 8-30: **Unclip the screen's ribbon cable.**

Connector

9. Remove the logic board from the iPod (see Figure 8-31).

10. Pull the screen from the iPod (see Figure 8-32). Only the logic board and the Click Wheel remain.

Figure 8-31: **Remove the logic board.**

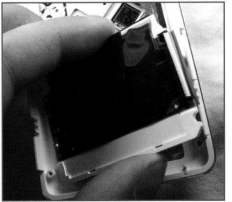

Figure 8-32: **Remove the screen.**

11. Put the screen into the new front panel.

12. Put the logic board into the new front panel.

13. Reconnect the screen to the logic board.

14. Reconnect the Click Wheel to the logic board.

15. Replace all the T6 Torx screws.

16. Plug the battery back into the logic board.

17. Replace the black tape over the hard drive connector.

18. Plug the audio jack back in.

19. Put the iPod back together.

Replace the Front Panel in an iPod Video

To replace the front panel in a fifth-generation iPod:

1. Open the iPod according to the instructions in Chapter 3.

2. At the bottom of the unit, find and disconnect the ribbon cable from the battery (see Figure 8-33). There is a brown clip that you can pull up to make the cable easier to remove. Be gentle with this clip, though, as it can pop off. Also, grip the cable near the connector, not where you see the fingers in the figure.

3. Find and disconnect the ribbon cable from the audio jack (see Figure 8-34). This connector also has a brown clip that works like the one in step 2.

Figure 8-34: **Remove the audio jack cable.**

4. Carefully lift the hard drive, disconnect it using the black clip (which works just like the brown clips from the previous steps), and remove it (see Figure 8-35).

5. Notice the six Phillips-head screws—three on each side—that hold the front panel of the iPod to the frame. Remove all six screws (see Figure 8-36).

6. Separate the front panel of the iPod from the screen and the logic board (see Figures 8-37 and 8-38).

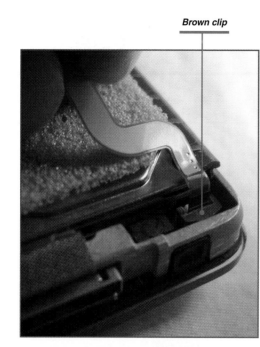

Brown clip

Figure 8-33: **Remove the battery cable.**

Figure 8-35: **Remove the hard drive.**

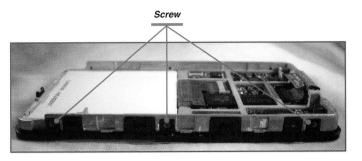

Figure 8-36: *Remove the screws.*

Figure 8-37: *Remove the front panel of the iPod.*

7. Put the new front panel onto the frame.

8. Replace the six Phillips-head screws.

9. Plug the hard drive back into the hard drive connector.

10. Reattach the audio jack ribbon cable into the connector on the logic board.

11. Rotate the hard drive, and place it in the iPod.

12. Plug the battery's ribbon cable back into the logic board.

13. Put the iPod back together.

Replace Your iPod Mini's Shell

Figure 8-38: *The front panel and the screen and logic board are now separated.*

For the iPod mini, you need to replace the entire shell, not just the front panel. See Table 8-3 for the required tools and the difficulty level.

iPOD MINI MODEL	TOOLS NEEDED	DIFFICULTY LEVEL
First-generation iPod mini	iPod-opening tools or flat-headed screwdriver and small Phillips-head screwdriver	Moderate
Second-generation iPod mini	iPod-opening tools or flat-headed screwdriver and small Phillips-head screwdriver	Moderate

Table 8-3: *Tools Needed and Difficulty Level for Replacing the iPod Mini's Shell*

To replace the shell of a first- or second-generation iPod mini:

1. Open the iPod mini according to the instructions in Chapter 3. The logic board and shell are now separate (see Figure 8-39).

Figure 8-39: **Separate the logic board and the shell.**

2. Slide the logic board into the new shell (see Figure 8-40).

Figure 8-40: **Put the logic board into the new shell.**

3. Plug the Click Wheel back into the logic board.

4. Put the screws back in the top.

5. Replace the metal clip at the bottom of the iPod mini.

Replace Your iPod Nano's Front Panel or Shell

The iPod nano is up to its old tricks, as Table 8-4 shows. For first-generation nanos, you replace the front panel, but for second-generation nanos, you replace the entire shell.

iPOD NANO MODEL	TASK	TOOLS NEEDED	DIFFICULTY LEVEL
First-generation iPod nano	Replace the front panel only	iPod-opening tools or flat-headed screwdriver and small Phillips-head screwdriver	Moderate
Second-generation iPod nano	Replace the entire shell	iPod-opening tools or flat-headed screwdriver and small Phillips-head screwdriver	Hard

Table 8-4: **Tools Needed and Difficulty Level for Replacing the Front Panel or Shell of an iPod Nano**

Replace the Front Panel in a First-Generation iPod Nano

To replace the front panel in a first-generation iPod nano:

1. Open the iPod nano according to the instructions in Chapter 3.

2. Three screws hold the logic board down. With your Phillips-head screwdriver, remove these screws (see Figure 8-41).

Screw ⊨

Figure 8-41: **Remove the screws.**

Figure 8-42: **Release the battery.**

3. Release the battery from the logic board (see Figure 8-42). Use your iPod-opening tool, because the battery is glued down. Do *not* completely remove the battery from the logic board, because it is soldered in place.

Figure 8-43: **Pull off the screen.**

4. Carefully pull the screen from the front panel (see Figure 8-43). The screen is glued down with adhesive.

5. Notice the ribbon cable that connects the front panel of the iPod nano to the logic board. Release the clip, and unplug this ribbon cable to free the logic board (see Figure 8-44). Then pull the logic board from the iPod nano. Now the front panel and the logic board are separate (see Figure 8-45).

6. Connect the new front panel to the logic board by attaching the Click Wheel's ribbon cable (see Figure 8-46).

Figure 8-44: **Remove the ribbon cable.**

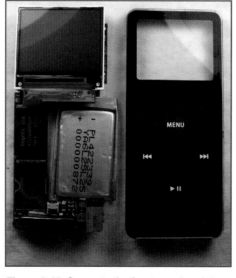

Figure 8-45: **Separate the front panel and the logic board.**

Figure 8-46: **Connect the new front panel to the logic board.**

7. Place the logic board back into the iPod nano.

8. Replace the three screws.

9. Put the iPod nano back together.

Replace the Shell in a Second-Generation iPod Nano

To replace the shell in a second-generation iPod nano:

1. Open the iPod nano according to the instructions in Chapter 3. The logic board and its contents are now separate from the shell (see Figure 8-47).

2. Carefully slide the logic board into the new shell (see Figure 8-48).

3. Reattach the audio jack to the logic board.

4. Replace the screw under the audio jack.

5. Place the metal bracket back into the bottom of the iPod nano.

6. Slide the audio jack back into place.

7. Replace the screws on the bottom and the top.

8. Put the top and bottom plastic pieces back into place.

Figure 8-47: Separate the shell from the insides of the iPod nano.

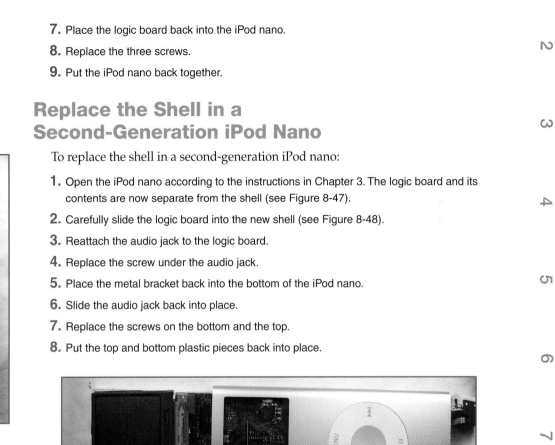

Figure 8-48: Slide the logic board into the new shell.

Chapter 9

Does Not Compute: Replacing the Logic Board

When your iPod was young, did life seem so wonderful? A miracle? Was it beautiful? Magical? That's because the logic board was working perfectly. But logic boards are components like any other, and they go bad from time to time. If yours is making you clinical, cynical, or fanatical because it's not so logical or dependable (in fact, it's a vegetable), replacing the logic board is the cure, as we show in this chapter. The cure to Supertramp, however, we have not yet discovered.

Check the Signs of a Bad Logic Board

The logic board is the brain of your iPod. No joke—your iPod is a miniature computer. The logic board contains the microprocessor as well as the connections to the various other components and systems: the battery, the hard drive or flash memory, the display, the audio, the data ports, and so on. If something goes wrong with your logic board, it's not unlike massive head trauma in a human.

NOTE

When one hears "The Logical Song" from Supertramp's 1979 album *Breakfast in America*, one wonders if it is some sort of joke. As it turns out, it sort of is. In the late 1960s, a Dutch millionaire, wanting to diversify his portfolio, offered to bankroll struggling keyboardist/singer Rick Davies if he put a band together. Davies didn't have to be asked twice. Thus was born Supertramp, the lounge act of the progressive rock era, who borrowed liberally from the likes of Procol Harum and Yes (not that you could tell once Davies and his main conspirator, Roger Hodgson, were finished with them). The first two Supertramp albums generated nothing but debt for Davies' patron. But the third album, 1974's *Crime of the Century*, found the trademark mix of Wurlitzer piano, pop melody, and proto-disco that would propel Supertramp to commercial success through the rest of the decade.

QUICK**FACTS**

GETTING A NEW LOGIC BOARD

You can buy a replacement logic board for your iPod at just about any iPod repair service. Don't know where to start? Do an Internet search, try eBay, or see Brandon at www.Synctogo.com.

Unfortunately, the logic board isn't the cheapest component to replace. Yours will cost you from $50 to $150 U.S., depending on your iPod. Once you factor in the cost of your labor, it might be cheaper for you just to buy a new iPod. On the other hand, if you do buy a new iPod, you'll need to transfer all your music files. Assuming that your hard drive is working fine, replacing the logic board in your current iPod saves you from that particular hassle.

A bad logic board reveals itself in different ways. Your iPod might not turn on, even when you plug it into a charger. If the iPod does turn on, it might show the sad face or the folder icon, or it might freeze on the Apple logo.

It's hard to diagnose a bad logic board from the symptoms alone, because they're the same symptoms that you get from other problems. Before you decide that the logic board is bad, be sure to rule out other possible causes. For instance, if the iPod doesn't turn on, check out the battery, or if you get the folder icon, you might want to look into the hard drive or the software. Restoring your iPod in iTunes might do the trick.

When you're reasonably convinced that the other components are in good working order, the logic board looks more and more like the culprit.

Replace Your iPod's Logic Board

Table 9-1 shows the required tools and the difficulty level of replacing the logic board in an iPod. We talk about the iPod mini and the iPod nano in subsequent sections of this chapter.

iPOD MODEL	TOOLS NEEDED	DIFFICULTY LEVEL
First-generation iPod	iPod-opening tools or flat-headed screwdriver and T6 Torx screwdriver	Moderate
Second-generation iPod	iPod-opening tools or flat-headed screwdriver and T6 Torx screwdriver	Moderate
Third-generation iPod	iPod-opening tools or flat-headed screwdriver and T6 Torx screwdriver	Moderate
Fourth-generation iPod (monochrome)	iPod-opening tools or flat-headed screwdriver and T6 Torx screwdriver	Moderate
iPod photo (fourth-generation color iPod)	iPod-opening tools or flat-headed screwdriver and T6 Torx screwdriver	Moderate
iPod video (fifth-generation iPod)	iPod-opening tools or flat-headed screwdriver and small Phillips-head screwdriver	Hard

*Table 9-1: **Tools Needed and Difficulty Level for Replacing the Logic Board in an iPod***

Figure 9-1: *Pull the battery from the hard drive.*

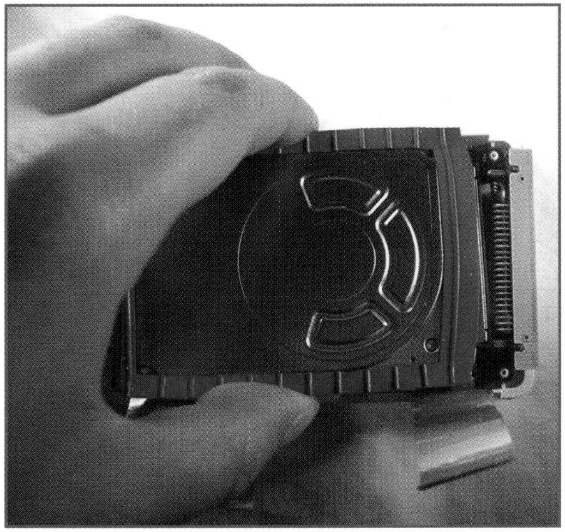

Replace the Logic Board in a First-Generation iPod

To replace the logic board in a first-generation iPod:

1. Open the iPod according to the instructions in Chapter 3.
2. Pull the battery from the back of the hard drive (see Figure 9-1). There is adhesive holding it down.
3. Unplug the battery from the logic board (see Figure 9-2).

Figure 9-2: *Unplug the battery.*

4. Carefully slide the hard drive from the orange hard drive connector.
5. Pull the hard drive from the iPod (see Figure 9-3).
6. Find the four T6 Torx screws in the logic board. A large piece of rubber covers one of them. Remove this piece of rubber to expose the fourth screw (see Figure 9-4).
7. With your T6 Torx screwdriver, remove all four screws (see Figure 9-5).

Figure 9-3: *Pull out the hard drive.*

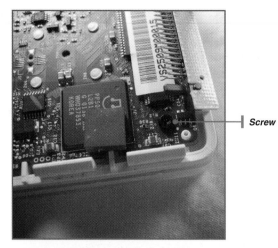

Figure 9-4: *Remove the piece of rubber to expose the fourth T6 Torx screw.*

Screw

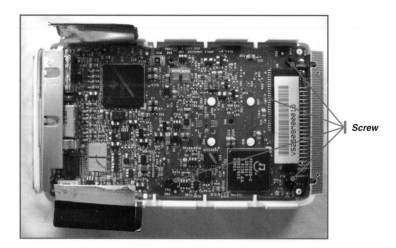

Figure 9-5: *Remove the T6 Torx screws.*

Screw

8. Remove the logic board from the bottom of the iPod (see Figure 9-6).

9. The screen has four white clips: two on each side of the logic board. These clips hold the screen in place. Disconnect them (see Figure 9-7).

Figure 9-6: *Remove the logic board.*

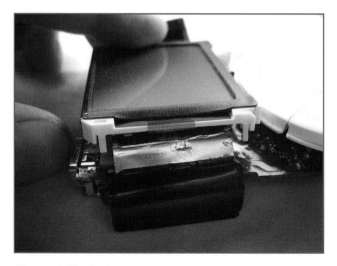

Figure 9-7: *Unclip the screen.*

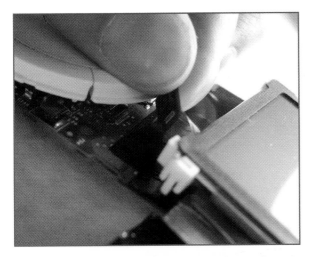

*Figure 9-8: **Unplug the screen from the logic board.***

10. Find the connector for the screen underneath the Click Wheel. Carefully unplug this connector with your iPod-opening tool or small flat-headed screwdriver (see Figure 9-8).

11. Connect the screen to the new logic board.

12. Connect the four white clips, and make sure they're holding the screen in place.

13. Fasten the four T6 Torx screws to the new logic board.

14. Slide the hard drive into the hard drive connector.

15. Plug the battery into the new logic board.

16. Put the iPod back together.

Replace the Logic Board in a Second-Generation iPod

To replace the logic board in a second-generation iPod:

1. Open the iPod according to the instructions in Chapter 3.

2. Pull the battery from the back of the hard drive. There is adhesive holding it down.

3. Unplug the battery from the logic board.

4. Carefully slide the hard drive from the orange hard drive connector.

5. Notice the two small brown clips next to the hard drive connector. Pull down on them gently to loosen the connector, and remove it from the logic board (see Figure 9-9).

6. Pull the piece of blue rubber from the iPod.

7. Loosen the scroll wheel's connector by pulling down on the brown tabs, just like you did with the hard drive connector in step 5 (see Figure 9-10).

*Figure 9-9: **Remove the hard drive connector.***

*Figure 9-10: **Loosen the scroll wheel's connector.***

Figure 9-11: *Remove the T6 Torx screws.*

8. Remove all eight T6 Torx screws from the logic board (see Figure 9-11).

9. Carefully lift the logic board just enough to release the scroll wheel's connector (see Figure 9-12).

Screw

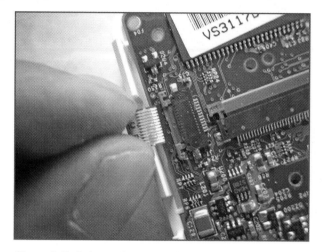

Figure 9-12: *Release the scroll wheel's connector.*

10. Remove the logic board (see Figure 9-13).

11. Release the white side clips holding the screen to the logic board (see Figure 9-14).

Figure 9-13: *Remove the logic board.*

Figure 9-14: *Unclip the screen.*

Figure 9-15: **Unplug the screen from the logic board.**

12. Carefully unplug the connector holding the screen to the logic board (see Figure 9-15).

13. Connect the screen to the new logic board.

14. Place the new logic board in the iPod, and screw in all eight T6 Torx screws.

15. Plug in the scroll wheel's ribbon cable.

16. Reattach the hard drive connector, and place the piece of blue rubber where you found it.

17. Slide the hard drive into place.

18. Plug the battery into the new logic board, and place the battery on top of the hard drive.

19. Put the iPod back together.

Replace the Logic Board in a Third-Generation iPod

To replace the logic board in a third-generation iPod:

1. Open the iPod according to the instructions in Chapter 3.

2. Unplug the audio jack from the logic board.

3. Slide the hard drive from the hard drive connector, and remove the hard drive from the iPod (see Figure 9-16).

4. Unplug the hard drive connector from the logic board, and remove it from the iPod (see Figure 9-17).

Figure 9-16: **Remove the hard drive.**

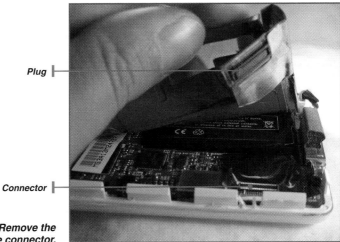

Plug

Connector

Figure 9-17: **Remove the hard drive connector.**

Figure 9-18: ***Unplug the battery.***

5. Unplug the battery from the logic board (see Figure 9-18).

6. Remove the battery from the iPod (see Figure 9-19).

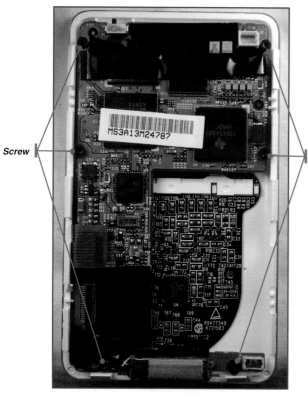

Screw **Screw**

Figure 9-20: ***Remove the T6 Torx screws.***

Figure 9-19: ***Remove the battery.***

7. With your T6 Torx screwdriver, remove all six screws from the logic board (see Figure 9-20).

8. Remove the logic board from the front of the iPod (see Figure 9-21). A connector holds the logic board in place. Just unplug it.

Connector

*Figure 9-21: **Remove the logic board.***

9. Plug the new logic board into the iPod.

10. Fasten the six T6 Torx screws to the new logic board.

11. Plug the battery into the new logic board.

12. Plug the hard drive connector into the new logic board.

13. Slide the hard drive back into the connector.

14. Plug the audio jack into the new logic board.

15. Snap the iPod back together.

Replace the Logic Board in a Fourth-Generation iPod or an iPod Photo

To replace the logic board in a fourth-generation monochrome iPod or an iPod photo:

1. Open the iPod according to the instructions in Chapter 3.

2. Unplug the audio jack from the logic board.

3. Slide the hard drive from the hard drive connector, and remove the hard drive from the iPod.

4. Unplug the battery from the logic board, and remove the battery (see Figure 9-22).

*Figure 9-22: **Remove the battery.***

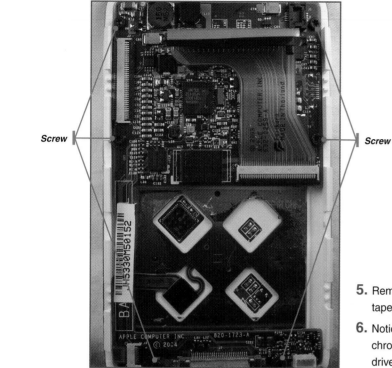

Screw   Screw

Figure 9-24: **Remove the T6 Torx screws.**

Figure 9-23: **Remove the tape.**

5. Remove the black tape covering the hard drive connector (see Figure 9-23). Keep the tape, however, because you'll need it later.

6. Notice the exposed T6 Torx screws. There are six of them in a fourth-generation mono-chrome iPod, and there are five of them in an iPod photo. With your T6 Torx screw-driver, remove them all (see Figure 9-24).

7. Unclip the ribbon cable connecting the Click Wheel to the logic board (see Figure 9-25). This is the ribbon cable on the bottom.

Figure 9-25: **Unclip the Click Wheel's ribbon cable.**

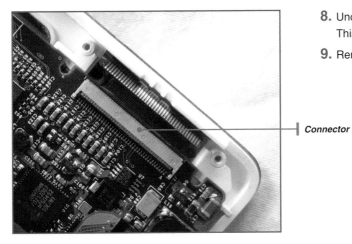

Figure 9-26: *Unclip the screen's ribbon cable.*

Connector

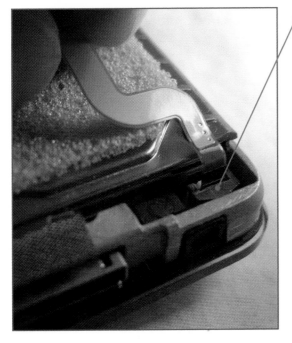

Brown clip

Figure 9-28: *Remove the battery cable.*

8. Unclip the ribbon cable connecting the screen to the logic board (see Figure 9-26). This is the ribbon cable on the top.

9. Remove the logic board from the iPod (see Figure 5-27).

Figure 9-27: *Remove the logic board.*

10. Put the new logic board in the iPod.

11. Connect the screen to the new logic board.

12. Connect the Click Wheel to the new logic board.

13. Fasten all the T6 Torx screws to the new logic board.

14. Plug the battery into the new logic board.

15. Replace the black tape over the hard drive connector.

16. Plug the audio jack into the new logic board.

17. Put the iPod back together.

Replace the Logic Board in an iPod Video

To replace the logic board in a fifth-generation iPod:

1. Open the iPod according to the instructions in Chapter 3.

2. At the bottom of the unit, find and disconnect the ribbon cable from the battery (see Figure 9-28). There is a brown clip that you can pull up to make the cable easier to remove. Be gentle with this clip, because it can pop off.

Figure 9-29: *Remove the audio jack cable.*

3. Find and disconnect the ribbon cable from the audio jack (see Figure 9-29). This connector also has a brown clip that works like the one in step 2.

4. Carefully lift the hard drive and rotate it out of the iPod casing, disconnect it using the black clip (which works just like the brown clips from the previous steps), and remove it (see Figure 9-30).

Figure 9-30: *Remove the hard drive.*

5. Once the hard drive is removed, unclip the screen from the logic board (see Figure 9-31). Use the brown clip as needed.

6. Notice the six Phillips-head screws—three on each side—that hold the front panel of the iPod to the frame. Remove all six screws (see Figure 9-32).

Figure 9-31: *Unclip the screen.*

Screw

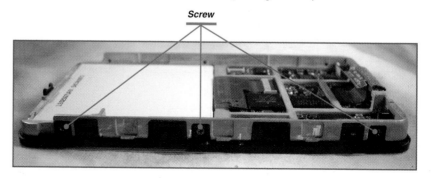

Figure 9-32: *Remove the screws.*

Figure 9-33: **Remove the front panel of the iPod.**

7. Separate the front panel of the iPod from the screen and the logic board (see Figure 9-33).

8. Pull the screen out of the logic board (see Figure 9-34).

Figure 9-34: **Remove the screen.**

9. Push the logic board out of the metal frame. There is a little piece of the ribbon cable from the Click Wheel stuck to the metal frame; you need to pull this up. Note also that the logic board is held down with adhesive (see Figure 9-35).

Figure 9-35: **Remove the logic board from the frame.**

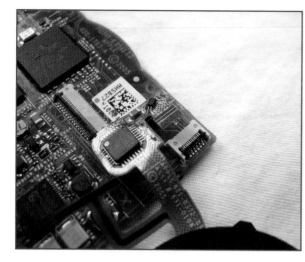

Figure 9-36: **Remove the Click Wheel from the logic board.**

10. Unplug the Click Wheel from the logic board (see Figure 9-36).

11. Connect the Click Wheel to the new logic board.

12. Place the new logic board in the frame.

13. Connect the screen to the new logic board.

14. Put the front panel of the iPod back onto the frame.

15. Replace the six Phillips-head screws.

16. Clip the screen's ribbon cable connector down.

17. Plug the hard drive back into the hard drive connector.

18. Attach the audio jack ribbon cable into the connector on the new logic board.

19. Rotate the hard drive, and place it in the iPod.

20. Plug the battery's ribbon cable into the new logic board.

21. Put the iPod back together.

Replace Your iPod Mini's Logic Board

Table 9-2 shows the tools needed and the difficulty level of replacing the logic board in an iPod mini.

To replace the logic board of a first- or second-generation iPod mini:

1. Open the iPod according to the instructions in Chapter 3.

2. Four clips—two per side—attach the screen to the iPod mini. Unclip them to release the screen (see Figure 9-37).

Figure 9-37: **Unclip the screen.**

iPOD MINI MODEL	TOOLS NEEDED	DIFFICULTY LEVEL
First-generation iPod mini	iPod-opening tools or flat-headed screwdriver and small Phillips-head screwdriver	Moderate
Second-generation iPod mini	iPod-opening tools or flat-headed screwdriver and small Phillips-head screwdriver	Moderate

Table 9-2: **Tools Needed and Difficulty Level for Replacing the Logic Board in an iPod Mini**

Cable   Connector

Figure 9-38: *Disconnect the screen's ribbon cable.*

3. The screen is connected to the logic board by a ribbon cable, which is slid into a small, brown clip. Release the brown clip, and the ribbon cable slides out easily (see Figure 9-38).

4. Unplug the battery from the logic board (see Figure 9-39).

5. Unplug the hard drive from the logic board (see Figure 9-40).

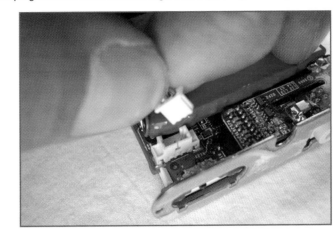

Figure 9-39: *Unplug the battery.*

Figure 9-40: *Unplug the hard drive.*

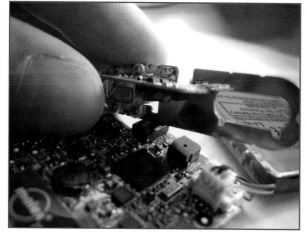

Figure 9-41: *Unplug the audio jack.*

6. Unplug the audio jack from the logic board (see Figure 9-41).

7. Plug the screen into the new logic board.

8. Plug the audio jack into the new logic board.

9. Plug the battery into the new logic board.

10. Plug the hard drive into the new logic board.

11. Slide the new logic board into the shell.

12. Plug the Click Wheel into the new logic board.

13. Put the screws back in the top.

14. Replace the metal clip at the bottom of the iPod mini.

15. Replace the plastic pieces on the top and bottom of the iPod mini.

Replace the Logic Board in a First-Generation iPod Nano

As you can see from Table 9-3, replacing the logic board in a first-generation iPod nano is just challenging enough to be interesting, but the second-generation nano is another story entirely. Unless you have a lot of experience fixing nanos, you shouldn't attempt to replace the logic board on your own. Find yourself an iPod repair service instead.

iPOD NANO MODEL	TOOLS NEEDED	DIFFICULTY LEVEL
First-generation iPod nano	iPod-opening tools or flat-headed screwdriver and small Phillips-head screwdriver	Moderate
Second-generation iPod nano	Not advised	Do not attempt

Table 9-3: *Tools Needed and Difficulty Level for Replacing the Logic Board in an iPod Nano*

To replace the logic board in a first-generation iPod nano:

1. Open the iPod according to the instructions in Chapter 3.

2. Three screws hold down the logic board. With your Phillips-head screwdriver, remove these screws (see Figure 9-42).

Screw

Figure 9-42: *Remove the screws.*

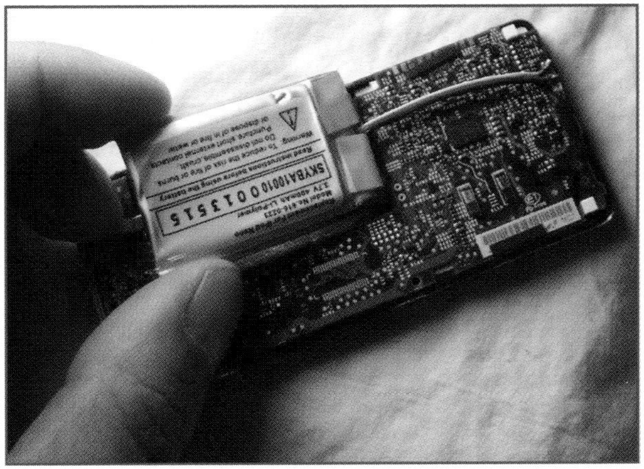

3. Release the battery from the logic board (see Figure 9-43). Use your iPod-opening tool, because the battery is glued down. Do *not* completely remove the battery from the logic board, because it is soldered in place.

4. Carefully pull the screen from the front panel (see Figure 9-44). The screen is glued down with adhesive.

Figure 9-43: *Release the battery.*

Figure 9-44: *Pull off the screen.*

Clip

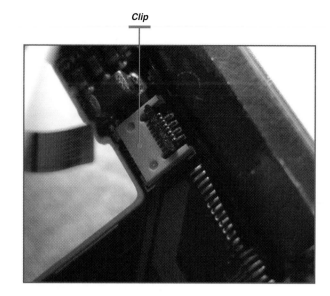

Figure 9-45: *Remove the ribbon cable, and pull out the logic board.*

5. A ribbon cable connects the front panel of the iPod nano to the logic board. Release the clip, and unplug this ribbon cable to free the logic board (see Figure 9-45). Then pull the logic board from the iPod nano.

6. Release the side clips that hold the screen to the logic board (see Figure 9-46). There are two on each side. You should be able to use your fingers.

7. Locate the ribbon cable that connects the screen to the logic board, and unclip it (see Figure 9-47).

Cable   Connector

Figure 9-47: *Disconnect the screen from the logic board.*

8. Attach the screen to the new logic board, and plug the ribbon cable into its connector.

9. Plug the Click Wheel's ribbon cable into the new logic board.

10. Place the new logic board into the iPod nano.

11. Fasten the three screws to the new logic board.

12. Put the iPod nano back together.

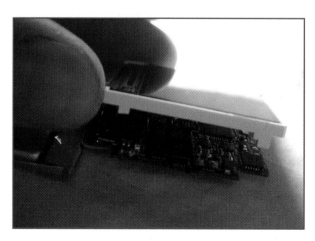

Figure 9-46: *Unclip the screen.*

Chapter 10

More Than Just Tunes: Looking at Third-Party Firmware and Software

We've spent nine whole chapters in this book talking about hardware fixes. Before we leave you, we thought we'd take you on a brief tour of the software side of the iPod equation.

Normally, when it comes to iPod software, you look no further than Apple's own iTunes. Maybe iTunes does everything you want it to do, but then again, maybe it doesn't. For instance, you might want an easier way to transfer your music files from your iPod to your computer. A couple of independent software companies have come up with solutions to that particular problem, which they provide alongside other iPod enhancements that are sure to be of interest.

We talk about those in the second half of this chapter. We start you off with trading up your iPod's operating system, for those of you who are so inclined.

Check Out iPodLinux

When most people come across a new handheld, hard drive–based consumer electronics device, they think about all the ways they can use it to improve the status or quality of their lives. There is that subset of people, however, for whom a new handheld, hard drive–based consumer electronics device isn't so much a ticket to Coolsville or Easy Street as it is an invitation to port a Linux kernel.

The people at the iPodLinux project are just this sort. They've managed to get a species of Linux—the popular open-source computer operating system—onto first-, second-, and third-generation iPods, with development ongoing for later models.

To a non-geek, this might seem like the ultimate so-what moment, but just take a minute to consider the possibilities. We've mentioned many times before that your iPod already has its own built-in operating system, or *firmware*, as it's called, but the iPod's firmware, as sophisticated as it is, is fairly limited as far as operating systems go, and your iPod has a lot more going for it than it lets on. Replacing your iPod's built-in operating system with something more robust—something like Linux, for example, which plays in the same league as Windows and Mac OS X—brings out your iPod's inner computer in ways that Steve Jobs never conceived of. You get your tunes—that's just a given—plus games, calculators, calendars, clocks, maps, text editors, graphics editors, system utilities, and on and on. Suddenly you're not just packing an MP3 player. You've got a surprisingly versatile digital engine of computation right there in the palm of your hand.

NOTE

iPodLinux is not the only alternate firmware that you can install and use on your iPod. If this sort of thing piques your fancy, you might also want to check out Rockbox (www.rockbox.org). As this book goes to press, Rockbox installations support the iPod in all generations from the first to the fifth; both generations of the iPod mini; and the first-generation iPod nano; among many other brands of MP3 players.

So is iPodLinux going to render obsolete your personal digital assistant (PDA) or notebook computer? Probably not—at least not today. For serious business, you need more than just an iPod. Where iPodLinux really shines is in enhancing your iPod's entertainment value, not to mention your standing in your circle of friends. In a world where everyone else has the same old iPod, you certainly won't lose any peeing matches when you whip out your Linux-enhanced configuration.

You'll like the price, too. It's free of charge. Linux comes from the planet of open-source software, where *proprietary* is a dirty word and people work for the fun and glory of it, all for the simple pleasure of others, and iPodLinux is offered in the same community spirit.

The downside to iPodLinux is that it skews technical sometimes, particularly when something goes wrong. If you've never used Linux before, you might not know where to begin to fix whatever problems crop up. The iPodLinux project does offer technical support of a sort, although they are not a for-profit venture, so they're not in the business of being nice to customers who don't really know what they're doing. If you go to them with a general complaint, particularly with the mindset of the jilted consumer, "revenge of the nerds" doesn't quite cover the level of sarcasm that you will experience. Apple is even less help to you, because iPodLinux is operating way outside the traditional corporate comfort zone. Basically, if you get in over your head, it's on you.

You might wonder what can go wrong if you do switch to iPodLinux. The answer: everything, but only temporarily. Your iPod can stop working, and you might lose your music. However, it's not like a game of Russian roulette. If you take your time with the installation, you shouldn't have anything to worry about. And you improve your chances of success immensely by installing iPodLinux on older iPods only, no newer than the third generation.

Even if absolutely everything goes wrong, a good old-fashioned restore from iTunes will correct any problems that iPodLinux introduces. In no case does iPodLinux harm your iPod's hardware, so you'll always be able to go back to the original factory settings.

Before you attempt to install iPodLinux on your iPod, you want to read over the documentation thoroughly, which you find on the project's Web site at www.ipodlinux.org (see Figure 10-1). There is a good deal of it, so make yourself comfortable, and if you begin to experience that queasy feeling that you always used to get in algebra class, you might be better off giving iPodLinux a skip.

Figure 10-1: Check out iPodLinux on the Web.

Install iPodLinux

As we mentioned, the first step in getting iPodLinux is to point your Web browser to www.ipodlinux.org and read over the documentation.

When you're ready to continue, look for a link to the official installer. The installer is a software application that you download and run from your computer. There are three different versions: one for Windows XP, one for Mac OS X, and one for Linux. Choose the one that corresponds to your computer's operating system. So if you're on a computer running Windows XP, you want the Windows XP installer, even though your iPod is made by Apple.

After you've downloaded the installer application:

1. Double-click the installer's icon on your computer. The installer launches, as this illustration shows.

2. Connect your iPod to your computer.

3. Your iPod should enter Disk Mode automatically. (You know it's in Disk Mode when you see the Do Not Disconnect message.) If your iPod doesn't enter Disk Mode, you can always force it. See Chapter 2 for how to put your iPod into Disk Mode manually.

4. Select your iPod from the drop-down menu in the installer window, as this illustration shows.

```
○ ○ ○                    iPod–Linux Installer

iPod:  [ MELISSA'S I                                    ↕ ]

      ( Install   )   ☐ Make Linux Default OS
      ( Uninstall )

    Click the Install button to install Linux on this iPod.



    ( Eject iPod )                          ( Check For Updates )
```

5. Select the option to make Linux your default operating system if you want your iPod to boot up in iPodLinux instead of in the built-in Apple firmware, as the following illustration shows. If you don't select this option, you must choose which firmware to use whenever you turn on or reset your iPod.

```
○ ○ ○                    iPod–Linux Installer

iPod:  [ MELISSA'S I                                    ↕ ]

      ( Install   )   ☑ Make Linux Default OS
      ( Uninstall )

    Click the Install button to install Linux on this iPod.



    ( Eject iPod )                          ( Check For Updates )
```

TIP

If you choose to boot your iPod in iPodLinux automatically, you can switch back to the original Apple firmware by resetting the iPod and then holding down the **Rewind** button as the iPod boots up.

10

QUICKSTEPS

RECORD AUDIO WITH FACTORY EARBUDS

In iPodLinux, you can use the earbuds that came with your iPod to record audio directly to your iPod's hard drive, just like a tape recorder.

That might read like a misprint, but it isn't. Your earbuds are just very small speakers, as we've already pointed out. What you might not know, and which always blows minds when it's first learned, is that speakers and microphones are actually the same device. With the speaker, the sound comes out. With a microphone, the sound goes in. But the science behind them is exactly the same. That means that any speaker can double as a microphone, just like any microphone can double as a speaker. Your iPodLinux installation takes advantage of that fact to give you audio-recording capabilities right through your factory earbuds. You never need be misquoted again.

1. Connect your earbuds to the audio jack.

2. In podzilla, choose the **Extras** menu.

3. From the Extras menu, choose **Recordings**.

4. From the Recordings menu, choose **Mic Record**.

5. Press **Select** on your iPod to start recording. Use the **Play/Pause** button to pause.

6. Talk into the left earbud.

7. Press **Select** to stop recording.

8. Go to the Playback menu in podzilla to listen to your recording.

6. Click the Install button. Wait until the installation completely finishes before continuing.

7. Disconnect your iPod from your computer.

8. Reset your iPod by holding down the **Menu** and **Play** buttons for about five to eight seconds.

Congratulations! You're in iPodLinux. The graphical user interface, or GUI, of your new firmware is called podzilla after the Web browser Mozilla.

Feel free to explore. Your first stop might be some games. Try Steroids, your iPod Asteroids clone, or BlueCube, your iPod Tetris clone, among many others.

Check Out Anapod CopyGear

Anapod CopyGear is a standalone software application that enables you to transfer your music, photos, and videos from your iPod to your computer—a great way to make backups of all that valuable data (Marc, take note). Think of it as sort of an iTunes alternative. It's software for your computer, not firmware for your iPod, so you don't have to worry about your iPod's configuration. Plus, CopyGear works equally well with all iPod models.

You download CopyGear directly to your computer. Unlike iPodLinux, it's commercially licensed software, which means that you have to pay for your copy. How much you pay depends upon the version that you want. If you're using Mac OS X, you have only one choice: the Mac OS X version, which costs you $19.95 U.S. and works with every iPod ever made. Windows users have several options, ranging from $19.95 U.S. for the iPod shuffle version to $29.95 U.S. for the all-iPods-ever-made version. It's also worth noting that on computers running Windows, Anapod CopyGear comes as part of the Anapod Explorer bundle, which gives you buffed-up search and management features, while on a Mac, you get CopyGear only.

If you want to try before you buy, you can. Red Chair Software, the makers of the Anapod line, offer free trial versions for both Mac and Windows systems. Upgrade to a paid version, and you get free lifetime updates—not a bad incentive.

Get Anapod CopyGear

Point your Web browser to www.redchairsoftware.com/anapod (see Figure 10-2), and look for the link to Mac OS X software. Windows users, click the Get Anapod link instead. From this page, you can download the free trial version or supply

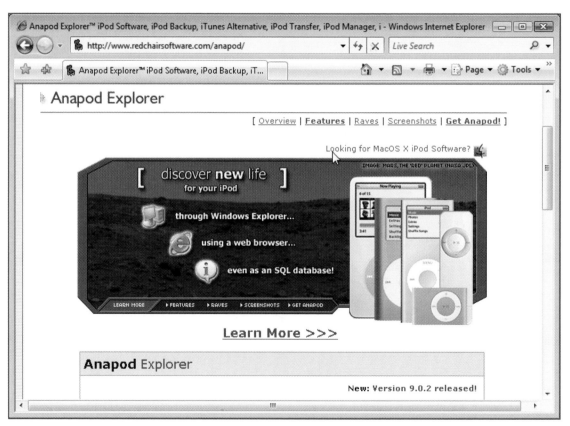

Figure 10-2: Get Anapod CopyGear (Mac OS X) or Anapod Explorer (Windows) on the Web.

your payment information and download the commercial version of your choice. To begin installation once the file has transferred, double-click the application's icon on your computer.

Copy Music Files with Anapod CopyGear

After you've installed Anapod CopyGear (or Anapod Explorer for Windows users), launch the application and connect your iPod to your computer. You see the contents of your iPod in the CopyGear window (see Figure 10-3).

CopyGear for Mac OS X			
Disconnect from iPod	/Volumes/MELISSA'S I		

iPod Contents	Copy Selected Items...	Select All	Invert Selection	Preferences...
Library				

Name	Type	Size	Length
– – 00 – 13Goingon30	mp4	809439 KB	97:43
– – 00 – 50 First Dates	mp4	467733 KB	99:04
– – 00 – Cheaper By the Dozen	mp4	466086 KB	98:45
– – 00 – Cheaper By the Dozen 2	mp4	442904 KB	93:51
– – 00 – Harry Potter Goblet Of Fire	mp4	610192 KB	156:55
– – 00 – HarryPotterandthesorceresstone	mp4	126172...	152:13
– – 00 – Hp Prisoner Of Azkaban Disc1	mp4	549988 KB	141:31
~ – 00 – Lucky_Number_Slevin	mp4	216854 KB	105:24
– – 00 – Marie Antoinette	mp4	567774 KB	124:28
– – 00 – Nanny McPhee	mp4	456957 KB	98:35
– – 00 – Over The Hedge	mp4	354887 KB	75:06
– – 00 – Pirates Of The Carribean	mp4	556151 KB	143:03
– – 00 – School for Scoundrels	mp4	507788 KB	107:41
– – 00 – She–s the Man	mp4	495626 KB	105:12
– – 00 – Sweet Home Alabama	mp4	512868 KB	108:48
– – 00 – TheLittleMermaid	mp4	682759 KB	82:37
– – 00 – Zathura	mp4	478121 KB	101:19
– – 00 – justmyluck	mp4	849910 KB	102:36
– – 00 – pirates of the Carabian 2	mp4	681913 KB	144:31
(+44) Feat. Carol Heller – When Your Hearts Stops Beating – 11 – Make You Smile	m4a	3562 KB	3:46
+44 – When Your Hearts Stops Beating – 01 – Lycanthrope	m4a	3811 KB	4:01
+44 – When Your Hearts Stops Beating – 02 – Baby Come On	m4a	2648 KB	2:48
+44 – When Your Hearts Stops Beating – 03 – When Your Heart Stops Beating	m4a	3100 KB	3:14
+44 – When Your Hearts Stops Beating – 04 – Little Death	m4a	3929 KB	4:07
+44 – When Your Hearts Stops Beating – 05 – 155	m4a	3362 KB	3:31
+44 – When Your Hearts Stops Beating – 06 – Lillian	m4a	4445 KB	4:40
+44 – When Your Hearts Stops Beating – 07 – Cliffdiving	m4a	3531 KB	3:42
+44 – When Your Hearts Stops Beating – 08 – Interlude	m4a	1185 KB	1:14
+44 – When Your Hearts Stops Beating – 09 – Weatherman	m4a	4350 KB	4:34
+44 – When Your Hearts Stops Beating – 10 – No, It Isn't	m4a	3402 KB	3:34
+44 – When Your Hearts Stops Beating – 12 – Chapter 13	m4a	4683 KB	5:09
+44 – When Your Hearts Stops Beating – 13 – Baby Come On (Acoustic)	m4a	2776 KB	2:54

Details

No tracks selected.

Figure 10-3: CopyGear shows the contents of your iPod.

To transfer music files back to your computer, select the files that you want to copy, and click the **Copy Selected Items** tab at the top of the interface. A pop-up window alerts you that file transfer is imminent, as the following illustration shows. Click the **Begin Copy** button to start copying.

Copy from iPod to Mac

Selected:	5 tracks.
Copy to:	/Users/brandonjones/Desktop (Change this folder in Preferences...)

Click 'Begin Copy' to start transfer.   (Begin Copy)

Summary:
   0 tracks copied successfully.
   0 tracks skipped because they already exist.
   0 tracks not copied due to error.

(Close)

Check Out iGadget

Another computer-based utility for copying your music files is iGadget from iPodSoft. In addition to creating computer backups of your iPod data, this software enables you to transfer all kinds of digital information to your iPod: daily horoscopes, driving directions, movie showtimes, and weather reports, plus Really Simple Syndication (RSS) feeds, podcasts, gas prices, and so on.

Like CopyGear, iGadget is direct-to-download software for your computer. You pay $15 U.S. for the Mac or Windows version. Unlike CopyGear, there is no free trial, although you can download a couple of free utilities from iPodSoft's Web site that mimic some of the features that you find in iGadget.

The software works on all versions of iPods. However, not all of the features are available on older iPods or the iPod shuffle. Newer iPods—third generation and on, plus the iPod mini and the iPod nano—give you the best results.

Get iGadget

Go to www.ipodsoft.com, and click the link for iGadget (see Figure 10-4). From this page, you can buy the Windows or Mac version of the software. You pay your money, and you download your iGadget. After the file transfers to your computer, double-click its icon to begin installation.

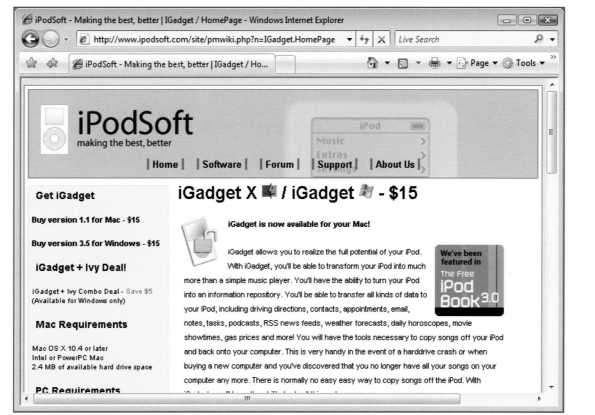

Figure 10-4: Get iGadget on the Web.

Important!
Avoid losing songs from your iPod.

Under certain circumstances, iTunes may delete all the songs off your iPod without you realizing it.

This can happen if the iPod is set to auto update with iTunes. If you no longer have your songs in iTunes and you connect the iPod again and it is set to auto update with iTunes, iTunes may erase all the songs from the iPod.

To prevent the iPod from automatically updating when you connect it to your computer, do the following:

Hold down Command–Option as you connect the iPod to your computer and continue holding these keys down until the iPod appears in the iTunes Source list.

OK

Copy Music Files with iGadget

When you launch iGadget for the first time, you see a pop-up window. On a Mac, the pop-up window explains how to prevent iTunes from auto-updating your iPod, as the illustration to the left shows. Be sure to read these instructions all the way through, because if iTunes auto-updates your iPod, you could end up losing your music.

On a Windows PC, the pop-up window asks you to disable iTunes temporarily to prevent iTunes from auto-updating your iPod and possibly deleting your music files. Select the option for this, and click **OK** to proceed.

Now connect your iPod to your computer. The software displays a screen like the one in Figure 10-5.

To copy music from your iPod to your computer, click the Transfer Songs plug-in on the left side of the interface window. In the Mac version of iGadget, it's right there in the open in the Plug-ins pane. In the Windows version, find the Transfer Songs From iPod plug-in under the iPod Information category.

Select the music files to copy by selecting the corresponding check boxes, and then click the **Transfer Songs** button in the toolbar along the top of the screen. A new window pops up, as the following illustration shows.

Select the parameters to use when transferring songs from the iPod to your PC and/or into iTunes.

Destination Folder:

~/Desktop   Choose...

☑ Transfer songs into iTunes

Space Information

| Required: | 17.08 MB (5 songs) |
| Available: | 36022.12 MB |

▶ Show advanced settings

Cancel   Transfer

10

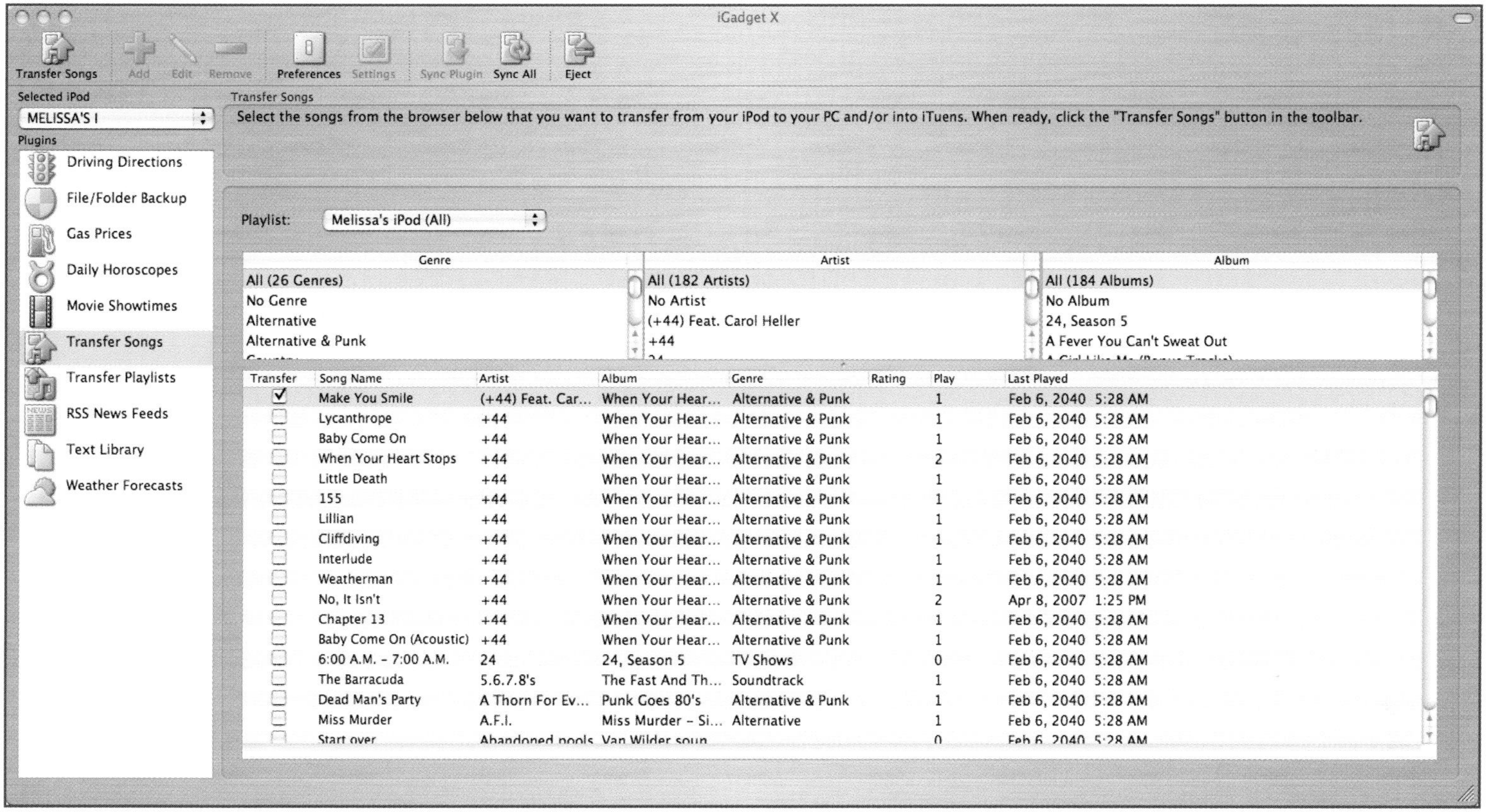

Figure 10-5: Welcome to iGadget!

Browse to the location on your computer where you'd like to save the copied files, and click the **Transfer** button.

Get Daily Horoscopes with iGadget

Avoid streaks of bad luck and karmic recalibrations with your daily guide to cosmic influence, right there in your iPod, courtesy of iGadget.

1. Mac users, choose the Daily Horoscopes plug-in from the pane on the left side of the interface window. Windows users, click the Internet Information category on the left side of the interface window, and choose the Daily Horoscopes plug-in.

2. Choose your sun sign and the dates of interest.

3. Click the **Sync Plug-in** button (Mac) or the **Sync Daily Horoscope** button (Windows).

You can now review the prophetic utterances of the planets in the Notes section of your iPod. Can't find your Notes section? Didn't know that you had one? Look under Extras in the main menu of your iPod.

Get Driving Directions with iGadget

Metaphysically isn't the only way for one to be lost. Assuming that your stars are in order, you want to make sure that the physical you is pointed in the right direction also. Get there fast on your iPod through iGadget.

1. Mac users, choose the Driving Directions plug-in from the pane on the left side of the interface window. Windows users, click the Internet Information category on the left side of the interface window, and choose the Driving Directions plug-in.

2. Click the **Add** button in the toolbar.

3. A pop-up window opens, as the following illustration shows. Enter your current location and your desired destination, and click **OK**.

Enter the locations between which you want driving directions.

Description of these directions

Starting Locatioin	Destination Locatioin
Address	Address
City, State or Zip / Postal Code	City, State or Zip / Postal Code
⦿ United States ◯ Canada	⦿ United States ◯ Canada

Cancel   OK

4. The pop-up window closes, and iGadget displays your driving directions. Select the ones to copy to your iPod.

5. Click the **Sync Plug-in** button (Mac) or the **Sync Driving Directions** button (Windows).

When you check your iPod's Notes or Contacts section, your driving directions should be there.

Get Movie Showtimes with iGadget

Missing work, school, deadlines, and meetings is life, but missing movies is unacceptable. Improve your ratio of timely arrival by carrying around showtimes in your iPod.

1. Mac users, choose the Movie Showtimes plug-in from the pane on the left side of the interface window. Windows users, click the Internet Information category on the left side of the interface window, and choose the Movie Showtimes plug-in.

2. Click the **Add** button in the toolbar.

3. A pop-up window opens, as the illustration to the left shows. Enter your current ZIP code, and type a brief description of this location—Home, Work, or Vacation, for example—for ease of reference later. Click **OK** to proceed.

4. The pop-up window closes, and iGadget displays the movie theaters in your area, along with the movies currently playing and the published showtimes. Select the desired results.

5. Click the **Sync Plug-in** button (Mac) or the **Sync Movie Showtimes** button (Windows).

Look in your iPod's Notes or Contacts section for the movies and showtimes.

Get Weather Forecasts with iGadget

Paul Simon gathers all the news he needs from the weather report. You can, too.

1. Mac users, choose the Weather Forecasts plug-in from the pane on the left side of the interface window. Windows users, click the Internet Information category on the left side of the interface window, and choose the Weather Forecasts plug-in.

2. Click the **Add** button in the toolbar.

3. A pop-up window opens, as the following illustration shows. Enter your current ZIP code or location ID, and type a quick description of this location. From the drop-down menu, choose the number of days to include in your forecast, and then click the option for metric or standard English (Imperial) units, depending on your preference. Click **OK** to continue.

Zip code (US only) or location id

What is a Location Id?

Go to weather.com and get your local forecast. Then, loo in the address line of your browser and note the value after the "/local/" text and before the question mark. That is your location id. This should look something like: GMXX0007

Description for this location

Forecast Days   3

Scale

○ Metric (celcius, meters, kph, etc.)
◉ Imperial (fahrenheit, miles, mph, etc.)

Cancel   OK

4. The pop-up window closes, and iGadget displays your weather reports. Select the ones to add to your iPod.

5. Click the **Sync Plug-in** button (Mac) or the **Sync Weather Report** button (Windows).

The weather reports appear in your iPod's Notes or Contacts section.

Number

5 In 1 option in diagnostic menu, function, 21

A

AAC (Advanced Audio Coding), 99–100
Advanced Audio Coding (AAC), 99–100
Anapod CopyGear software
 copying music files with, 149–150
 features of, 147–148
 getting, 148–149
Apple firmware, switching to, 146
Apple logo, unfreezing, 26
audio, recording with factory earbuds, 147
audio jack cable, removing to replace screen, 72
audio jacks
 checking, 93–94
 removing from iPod nano, 39–40
 replacing, 94–95, 99
 unplugging from iPod photo, 33
 unplugging to replace screen, 66, 68
Audio option in diagnostic menu, function, 21
audio quality versus storage space, 99–100
audio-jack replacement
 in fourth-generation iPods, 95–97
 in iPod minis, 99
 in iPod photos, 95–97
 in iPod videos, 97–99
 in third-generation iPods, 95–97

B

backups, making, 22
Batt A2D option in diagnostic menu, function, 21
batteries. *See also* low-battery; power
 charging, 23

checking, 44
checking connections in, 57
going bad, 44
impact of scanning hard drives on, 81
life of, 24
problems with, 44
prolonging lives of, 44
releasing for screen replacement in iPod
 nanos, 76
removing to replace screen, 67–68
unplugging for screen replacement, 60
unplugging from logic board, 45
unplugging to replace screen, 67
battery cables, removing to replace screen, 71
battery replacement
 in first- and second generation iPods, 45–46
 in first-generation iPod nano, 56–57
 in fourth-generation iPod, 50–51
 in iPod mini, 53–56
 in iPod photo, 50–51
 in iPod video, 51–53
 in third-generation iPods, 47–50

C

CF (CompactFlash) slot, relationship to
 Microdrive, 9
chargers, using with batteries, 24
Chgr Curr option in diagnostic menu,
 function, 21
Click Wheel, 11, 70
Click Wheel connector, unplugging from
 iPod mini, 36
CompactFlash (CF) slot, relationship to
 Microdrive, 9
compression, 99
Contrast option in diagnostic menu, function, 21

D

Daily Horoscope plug-in, using with iGadget,
 153–154
diagnostic menu
 accessing, 18–20
 navigating, 18
 options, 21
Disk Mode, iPod mini in, 91
Diskmode option in diagnostic menu,
 function, 21
drives. *See* hard drives
driving directions, getting with iGadget, 154–155
Drv Temp option in diagnostic menu, function, 21

E

earbuds, recording audio with, 147

F

factory earbuds, recording audio with, 147
fifth-generation iPods. *See also* iPods
 identifying, 8–9
 opening, 33–34
Figures
 diagnostic menu on newer iPods, 19–20
 diagnostic menu on older iPods, 18–19
 folder icon, 22
 low-battery icon, 24
 low-battery symbol, 25
 sad face, 21
Figures for fifth-generation iPods, features, 9
Figures for first-generation iPod nanos
 battery replacement, 56–57
 features, 13
 front-panel replacement, 119–121
 logic-board replacement, 138–140